# SS: THE SECRET ARCHIVES

# EASTERN FRONT

# SS: THE SECRET ARCHIVES

# EASTERN FRONT

### IAN BAXTER

**BARRON'S**

First edition for the United States, its territories
and dependencies and Canada, published in
2003 by Barron's Educational Series, Inc.

*All inquiries should be addressed to:*
Barron's Educational Series, Inc.
250 Wireless Boulevard
Hauppauge, NY 11788
**www.barronseduc.com**

*Library of Congress Catalog Card Number 2003107496.*

International Standard Book Number 0-7641-5672-1


Editorial and design by
Amber Books Ltd
Bradley's Close
74–77 White Lion Street
London N1 9PF
www.amberbooks.co.uk

Picture Credits:

A special thankyou goes to Richard White and Martin Kaludow for providing
some of the photographs in this volume.

All other images in this book are credited to the HITM ARCHIVE.

www.militaria-net.co.uk/hitm.htm

Dedicated to Michelle

Printed and bound in Italy by: Eurolitho S.p.A., Cesano Boscone (MI)

9 8 7 6 5 4 3 2 1

# CONTENTS

# OPERATION BARBAROSSA

On 22 June 1941, three German Army groups launched Adolf Hitler's attack on the Soviet Union. Included in this massive array of military might were the 160,405 soldiers of the *Waffen-SS*.

Most *SS* soldiers regarded the war with Russia as a holy crusade against Bolshevism and sub-humanity. Although the *SS* fought in every theatre of operations except Africa, it would be here, across this vast sprawling land, that they would fight the hardest and most fanatically. It would also be here in Russia that the *Waffen-SS* developed new fighting techniques unproven in any other theatres of war. Their belief in Nazi ideology was a key factor of their ruthlessness on the battlefield. Each soldier went to war against the Red Army believing that he was a member of a racial and biological elite. And to enable *SS* soldiers to carry out their tasks, no matter how distasteful or difficult, strict discipline meant that he would undertake every order issued by the *Führer* or given by his superior, regardless of the sacrifice. Although a

LEFT: *Totenkopf* troops in action, armed with a light 7.5cm (2.95in) Infantry Gun 18. It was not until 24–25 June 1941 that the division managed to clear the Lithuanian forests around Jurbarkas and move towards the Dvina for its opening attack in Operation *Barbarossa*. Just two days later the men of the *Totenkopf* became embroiled in vicious fighting with suicidal Red Army forces.

number of *SS* soldiers did not share a measure of the *Reichsführer's* ideological views, the zeal with which the bulk of the *SS* pursued the war against Russia suggests that many of them did.

But the *Waffen-SS* determination and combat effectiveness during those opening days of 'Barbarossa' was not solely based on ideological conviction. It was good training, effective leadership, and first-class armament that made the *SS* a crack branch of Hitler's military elite. These soldiers were without doubt a superior military formation, and were now employing their skill and fanaticism against an enemy which they had long regarded as sub-human.

Within hours of the initial invasion of Russia, the German spearheads, with their brilliant co-ordination of all arms, had pulverized bewildered Russian border formations into submission. The *Waffen-SS* commanders looked upon these first exhilarating days of the campaign as confirming the aura of invincibility that had not been enjoyed by any other army since Napoleon had unleashed his forces against Russia.

Initially the *Totenkopf* Division was not used for the opening strike against Russia, but within 48 hours it advanced at an incredible pace, covering Manstein's furious drive on the left flank. By 30 June, the *Totenkopf* reached Dvinsk and spent almost a week mopping up the battered remnants of the withdrawing Soviet units. The *Totenkopf*'s line of advance soon took it through Latvia, where on 2 July it ran into some stiff opposition. Only with the help of *Luftwaffe* support was the town eventually captured. Slowly the division continued to battle forward against stubborn resistance. From mid-July to late August, the *Totenkopf* was once again engaged in fierce, unremitting fighting against Soviet troops in heavily wooded and marshy terrain around Leningrad.

Meanwhile in Army Group Centre, both *Wehrmacht* and *Waffen-SS* troops, spearheaded by the 2nd and 3rd *Panzergruppe,* penetrated through Belarussia almost as far as Smolensk, a sprawling city on the Warsaw–Moscow highway. When they reached the city, they stood a mere 640km (400 miles) from the greatest prize of them all – Moscow. It was in this region in late July that *Das Reich* saw extensive action on the left flank of the Yelnya salient. Despite the relentless Soviet counterattacks, which saw the *Das Reich* Division nearly on the point of disintegration, it continued fighting until eventually withdrawing north of Smolensk to recuperate on 8 August. After this brief respite, the *Das Reich* Division went back into action and participated in an ambitious offensive that became one of the greatest victories, in numerical terms, in history.

## 'We only have to kick in the door, and the whole rotten Russian edifice will come tumbling down'
### Adolf Hitler

The triumphs came with the obliteration of five enemy armies in the Kiev pocket. It was here at Kiev that the *Das Reich* Division distinguished itself fighting in the encirclement of the city. By the time the surviving Soviet forces trapped in Kiev surrendered, the Red Army had lost nearly a million men killed, wounded, or captured.

With Kiev in enemy hands, the Germans were now in a good position to seize the strategically important oil-producing Caucasus Mountains and the Donets Basin with its industrialized areas. However, by mid-September Hitler began drawing up plans for the resumption of operations against Moscow. The regroup for the final assault on the Russian capital was a massive logistical nightmare, as General Guderian's *Panzergruppe* had to make the long haul back from the Ukraine, whilst General Hoeppner's tanks transferred from the Leningrad Front. Within two weeks, the forces of Army Group Centre, commanded by Field Marshal Fedor von Bock, were in place and ready for action. Most were confident, but a few officers looked askance at the calendar, worried about the coming onset of the ferocious Russian winter.

During the early hours of 30 September 1941, the first phase of Operation *Typhoon*, the attack on Moscow, began. Guderian's *Panzergruppe*, with *Das Reich* forming part of the armoured spearhead, was launched northeastwards towards Orel, from where it would thrust north behind Yeremenko's Bryansk Front. Two days later, on 2 October, the rest of the Army Group rolled forward with more than 2000 tanks to bear down on the Soviet capital. For the *Waffen-SS* taking part in this operation, it was truly an historic moment. *Das Reich* successfully completed its task of breaking through onto the main Smolensk–Moscow highway, and then captured Gshatsk after fierce fighting in the surrounding woods. The Red Army continued resisting to the death and frantically attempted to build up its forces in preparation to retake the town of Gshatsk. However, these Soviet efforts were blunted by determined attacks by the division's *Der Führer* Regiment.

The *Das Reich* Division continued advancing to Moscow, but against increasing opposition. Across the battlefield, both the *Wehrmacht* and *Waffen-SS* became locked in a battle of attrition with the Soviets, with intense and savage fighting in many areas. Along the smouldering front, the Soviets saturated vast areas with millions of high-explosive shells. Hundreds of new truck-mounted multiple rocket launchers, concealed under heavy camouflage, were brought into action, firing thousands of deadly salvos in quick succession into the advancing German lines. Even the most combat-hardened *SS* troops found the Soviet resistance hard going. To make matters worse, the weather began to change on 6 October as cold-driving rain fell on Army Group Centre's front. Within hours, the Russian countryside had been turned into a quagmire with roads and fields becoming virtually impassable. All the roads leading to Moscow had become boggy swamps.

Although tanks and other tracked vehicles managed to push through the mire, trucks and wheeled vehicles were hopelessly stuck up to their axles in deep boggy mud. That night, *SS* soldiers shivered for the first time as the rain turned to snow. The advance had gone from a glorious display of military might to a slow, pitiful slog eastward. Gradually, towards the end of October and into early November 1941, every German commander came to understand that 'Barbarossa' would not defeat the Red Army before the winter weather intervened.

The *Waffen-SS* had achieved spectacular victories. Its members had once again showed themselves to be fanatical soldiers, and on more than one occasion had shattered overwhelming enemy resistance. But the *Waffen-SS*, like the *Wehrmacht*, had suffered massive losses in both men and materiel. And now, poised in front of Moscow and Leningrad, the weather deteriorated. A winter war in Russia was inevitable.

RIGHT: A group of *Waffen-SS* soldiers pose for the camera during the early stages of the invasion of Russia in June 1941. To these *SS* men, the war with Russia was looked upon as a kind of holy crusade against Bolshevism and the 'sub-human' Slavs. Nazi ideology called on true 'Aryans' like these to eliminate all racially and biologically inferior elements, and to create what they saw as a 'good blood', which would be able to serve Germany to the best of its ability. The *Waffen-SS* felt that the war in the East was, unlike the fighting in the West, a conflict of ideologies. It was for this reason that most *SS* soldiers fought with a blend of determination and murderous ruthlessness that was to become the norm on the Eastern Front. Although atrocities occcured in the West, they were on a very minor scale compared to events in the East.

LEFT: During vicious fighting on the Eastern Front, a *Waffen-SS* soldier armed with a flame thrower captures a nervous Soviet soldier. Note how well the other *SS* troops blend in with the local terrain in their summer camouflage smocks. In June and July 1941, *SS* troops along with their *Wehrmacht* counterparts raced across the steppes of Russia, battering Red Army formations into submission. Those ravaged enemy divisions that were left intact withdrew in panic and disorder. The speed and power of the German drive across the Soviet heartland had given each soldier a feeling of invincibility, though this did not last. As they advanced deeper into Russia, Soviet resistance grew as the Red Army traded space for time, and German casualties increased.

ABOVE: Advancing *Waffen-SS* troops pass a burning Soviet tank during the initial phases of 'Barbarossa' – the code word for the invasion of Russia. Being Hitler's chosen spearhead troops, the *Waffen-SS* had immediate opportunities to distinguish themselves on the battlefield. With handpicked personnel, excellent training, effective leadership and first-class armament, they were a mix of either fanatics or skilful and courageous soldiers. The first *SS* divisions – *Leibstandarte*, *Das Reich* and *Totenkopf* – had by now been joined by the 5th *SS* Division *Wiking*, which was to amass a fighting reputation second-to-none in the East.

RIGHT: *Das Reich, Totenkopf, Wiking* and the *Polizei* Division were all components of *Generalfeldmarschall* Fedor von Bock's Army Group Centre. A Pz.Kpfw.III belonging to the *Das Reich* Division is seen here moving along Highway 1 during its drive on Moscow in 1941. By July, Bock had no more than 145 combat-worthy tanks remaining: his Panzer force had been worn down, not by the Red Army, but by the distances they had covered on bad roads. Nevertheless, the Germans continued to attack, stretching their supply lines to the limit. In the last weeks of July and early August, Army Group Centre's forces continued to fight over seemingly endless steppes, through huge forests, along dusty roads, and through the mud and mire when summer thunderstorms turned the land into bog. Still they continued pushing forward, forcing their way across numerous rivers and streams, and capturing thousands of Soviet soldiers, either in direct frontal assaults or in vast pincer movements.

BOTTOM RIGHT: A group of *Waffen-SS* men resting in a captured Soviet trench near the Sluczk river in 1941. They are members of the *Leibstandarte*, part of *Generalfeldmarschall* Gerd von Rundstedt's Army Group South. The *Leibstandarte* was deeply embroiled in the battles in western Ukraine. The division's drive had been rapid in spite of meeting spirited resistance. It fought against Soviet tank units trying to cut the Northern Highway at Dubno and Olyka and successfully drove them back. By 7 July 1941, it had reached Ostrog. Leading units crossed the river Sluczk, burst out of the bridgehead, smashed through the defences of the Stalin Line at Miropol and drove at breakneck speed towards Zhitomir.

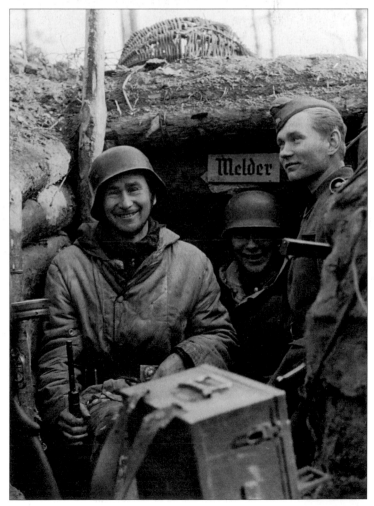

LEFT: *Leibstandarte* troops follow armoured vehicles through a corn field in southern Russia. Fighting had often been hard and bitter, with some Red Army forces doggedly resisting the invaders. But others offered very little opposition, and the division continued pressing forwards, almost invariably being rushed into the line to bolster the 1st Panzer Group. In some sectors of the front, especially when the *Leibstandarte* fought to capture the important Kudnov road junction, there were savage scenes of hand-to-hand fighting. From this point in the advance, every *SS* thrust encountered a Soviet counter-thrust, nearly every strike was met by fanatical resistance, and every attempt at a pincer movement found Soviet units attempting their own outflanking moves.

ABOVE: A *Leibstandarte* Panzer commander observes a burning Soviet T-34 tank that has just been knocked out by an 8.8cm (3.45in) Flak gun, known as the '88'. In spite of the massive Soviet tank losses incurred during the first two months of the campaign, Red Army tank replacements soon began reaching the battlefield. These included the excellent T-34. With its well-sloped armour, wide tracks and powerful gun, the T-34 was a match for any German tank, and it was virtually immune to most standard German anti-tank weapons. Only the powerful '88', which the *Waffen-SS* had clamoured for in 1941, could knock out the T-34 and even heavier KV-1 tanks, and German troops quickly developed a healthy respect for Soviet armour.

LEFT: In action in a burning Russian village, a German infantryman calls more troops forward to help repel dogged Red Army resistance. The soldier is armed with a captured Soviet PPSh-41 submachine gun, which many *Wehrmacht* and *Waffen-SS* troops preferred to the German MP-40. The PPSh was relatively crudely manufactured, but it was extremely tough and could be relied upon to work in the worst of conditions. It weighed 3.5kg (7lb 13oz) and could be fed either from a 71-round drum as seen here, or from a 35-round box magazine. It was capable of firing 900 rounds per minute. This photograph was taken during the drive by Army Group Centre, passing through the town of Gorki. It was not until 14 July 1941, after heavy fighting and considerable losses, that the *Das Reich* Division accompanied by the 10th *Panzer* Division reached the town. The following day, both divisions drove on past Smolensk to reach the River Yelnya. The Germans then held the river crossing for nearly a week while follow-on units caught up with the armoured force after its rapid advance eastward.

ABOVE: More Red Army troops are captured by the *Das Reich* Division during operations in Army Group Centre in July 1941. During this period, great victories beckoned for the invaders. On 9 July the town of Vitebsk was captured, and six days later a break-through in the centre saw the massive encirclement and the fall of the city of Smolensk. This effectively cut off a massive Soviet concentration of 300,000 troops between Orsha and Smolensk. These impressive gains,

however, counted for little because the *Das Reich* Division soon encountered terrible problems with the road system. The German advance was designed for mobile warfare on good roads supported by extensive railway systems. But here in the Soviet Union there were few all-weather roads and hardly any main railway lines. The *Das Reich* Division was thus compelled to move across country, and the dry sandy soil in the region slowed their advance to a crawl.

LEFT: A *Das Reich* motorcycle combination assists in the rounding-up of captured Soviet soldiers in what became the largest encirclement battle in the history of warfare. These troops belong to the motorcycle battalion of the *Der Führer* Regiment operating ahead of the main body of the *Das Reich* Division as it reached the battle zone. The attack was mounted on 6 September 1941, when the motorcycle battalion was ordered to raid and seize an intact railway bridge at Makoshim. It was then to hold a bridgehead on the south bank of the River Desna. The enemy had in fact prepared the bridge for demolition, but the motorcycle battalion risked their lives, racing across the bridge before it was blown. Engineers moved slowly forward cutting the detonating wires and taking away the high-explosive charges. The bridge was captured and an *SS* perimeter was established on the south bank.

ABOVE: Two *Das Reich* riflemen round up a number of Soviet prisoners. On 15 September 1941, Field Marshal von Bock noted the great achievements of the men of the *Das Reich* Division. 'An encircling ring had been flung around the Russians, but now the area had been significantly reduced against an enemy that was determined to smash its way out. The Russians have employed no fewer than three infantry divisions, two cavalry divisions and two tank brigades in one single effort, and on another sector of Corps front, at Putivl, the pupils of the Kharkov military academy, showing great skill and courage as they charged into the fire of *SS* machine-guns and died to the last man.'

BELOW: Within weeks, thousands of Soviet soldiers would be encircled in and around the city of Kiev. In that encirclement, five Soviet armies were totally destroyed and a further two severely battered. Almost a million Red Army soldiers had been killed, wounded or captured. Soviet forces in Army Group South had been all but annihilated, and the road to the great industrial area of the Donets Basin and oil-producing region of the Caucasus had now been laid open for a determined German thrust. However, the Kiev encirclement had required the diversion of Guderian's panzers from Army Group Centre, which meant that the drive on Moscow had been fatally delayed.

ABOVE: A cemetery of soldiers belonging to the 4th *SS Polizei* Division. The division was in Army Group North reserve during the opening phases of Operation *Barbarossa*, but by August 1941 it had been fully committed to the fighting. When the division was released from reserve, it saw heavy combat on the Leningrad front, losing more than 2000 men at Luga in July and losing a similar number a month later. By the end of the year, the *Polizei* Division was in combat on the Wolchow river, suffering further heavy loss.

RIGHT: Three major factors affected battle on the Eastern Front. The sheer size of Russia was beyond the experience of troops from Western Europe. Communications were made much harder by the poor quality of the road and rail system, which put enormous strain on the German logistics effort. And finally, the weather was a challenge: hot, dry and dusty in summer, with bottomless mud in spring and autumn, then cold beyond belief in winter.

BELOW: German troops on parade after taking a Russian town in the summer of 1941. The Soviet Union had not been a kindly master for many of its constituent republics: the Germans were greeted as liberators in parts of Belorussia, the Ukraine and the Baltic states. However the Nazis, with their contempt for the Slavs, wasted an opportunity. Behind the armies came the death squads of the *SS* and *SD Einsatzgruppen*, whose murderous activities turned potential allies into hostile partisans.

RIGHT: The field headquarters of the *Das Reich* Division just before the opening of *Barbarossa*. Note the heavily camouflaged vehicles concealed in the undergrowth. As had happened in France, the division had no major role during the operation's opening phase, and its component regiments were split up and used for security duties. When it did go into action, *Das Reich* quickly gained a reputation as a formidable fighting machine. In five months, the hard-fighting *SS* men had fought their way to the very edge of Moscow, within sight of the Kremlin. But tough though they were, they were not prepared for the fiercest of all Russian commanders – 'General Winter'.

LEFT: Soldiers of the *Polizei* Division pay their respects to a *Wehrmacht* grave during a pause in the fighting on the Leningrad Front in September 1941. The division suffered heavy casualties, being reduced to the *Kampfgruppe-SS Polizei* by February 1942. In that month, the unit, which had at first been controlled by the *SS* but not an actual part of the *SS*, was integrated as the *SS-Polizei-Division*. Police uniforms and insignia were replaced with their *Waffen-SS* equivalents, although division members still wore the Police capbadge. It was later reformed and upgraded, becoming in 1943 the 4th *SS-Panzer-grenadier Division Polizei*.

**ABOVE:** A *Das Reich* soldier's grave, seen during the German drive on Moscow in early October 1941. The regrouping for the final assault on the Russian capital was a massive logistical nightmare, as three Panzer groups – 2nd (Guderian), 3rd (Hoth) and 4th (Hoeppner) – were to be used. Of these, Hoth's Panzer force was already in place, while Guderian's had to make the long haul back from the Ukraine, and Hoeppner's tanks transferred from the Leningrad Front. Within two weeks, Bock's forces were in place and ready for action. During the early hours of 30 September 1941, the first phase of Operation *Typhoon*, as the attack on Moscow was called, began.

The 2nd *Panzergruppe* was launched northeastwards towards Orel, from where it would thrust north behind Yeremenko's Bryansk Front. Two days later, on 2 October, the rest of the Army Group rolled forward, with more than 2000 tanks bearing down on Moscow. Two days after that, the *Das Reich* Division joined Operation *Typhoon* when its units moved into action alongside the 10th Panzer Division. On 15 October, the division captured the town of Borodino after fierce fighting. Driving onwards, the division reached Mozhaisk, just 80km (50 miles) from Moscow, on 19 October. *Das Reich* had suffered 7000 casualties – 60 percent of its combat strength – since June 1941.

RIGHT: An *SS* trooper examines the wing of a Soviet Sukhoi bomber wrecked on an airfield in the west of the USSR. Soviet tactical airpower was one of the first targets for the *Luftwaffe* after the invasion in June 1941. Junkers Ju 87 Stuka divebombers, together with Heinkel He 111 and Junkers Ju 88 medium bombers, hit most Soviet airfields in the first wave of attacks, destroying thousands of aircraft before they had a chance to leave the ground. They then switched roles, returning to provide close support of the advancing German divisions. *SS* units as well as *Wehrmacht* units were trained to work in cooperation with the *Luftwaffe*. That cooperation between the ground and the air was extremely important to the German way of war. Aircraft ranged ahead of the advancing panzer and panzergrenadier divisions, attacking strongpoints, bunkers, armoured formations and enemy troop concentrations.

LEFT: As the massed ranks of Germany's invasion force drove eastwards, they quickly overran the airfields wrecked by *Luftwaffe* attacks. The Red Air Force was large, and could have played a key role in stopping the Germans. However, it was caught completely by surprise, even though its commanders had received intelligence of the German attack. Stalin, convinced that Hitler was going to live up to the non-aggression pact he had signed with the Soviet Union, had expressly forbidden his air force commanders to order an increased state of readiness. As a result, the aircraft which might have blunted the *Wehrmacht's* spearheads were destroyed.

RIGHT: *SS* troops pass a destroyed BT-7 Soviet light tank while operating with Army Group North. The radio antenna around the turret indicate that it was a command tank. These soldiers probably belong to the *Polizei* Division. Since the *Polizei* Division was not one of the 'classic' *SS* divisions, it was at the end of the line when modern equipment was issued and, unlike the fully motorized *Leibstandarte*, *Totenkopf*, *Das Reich* and *Wiking*, was almost totally dependent on horses to move its artillery and equipment. The bulk of its infantry moved on foot at the pace of a soldier or of the plodding horse. Not until 1942, when it was reconstituted as a fully fledged *SS* formation, did the *SS-Polizei* Division receive a compliment of halftrack vehicles, armoured carriers and prime movers. In the meantime, these soldiers have used their initiative, pressing bicycles into service in order to cover long distances more quickly.

ABOVE: Soldiers of the *Polizei* Division move along a road that has been submerged following a heavy downpour in September 1941. Although the rain was liable to come at any time in Russia, the wet season began in October 1941 and lasted about five weeks. Autumnal rains alternated with freezing nights, a phenomenon known to Russians as the *rasputitza* (literally 'time without roads'). Most roads were dirt tracks that dissolved into a sticky quagmire, which even tanks were unable to handle. Germans on foot sank past the top of their jackboots. Horses sank to their bellies. Airfields became unusable. The mud could paralyze an advancing division: once held immobile, it was a sitting target for the Soviet armour, whose broader tracks coped more easily and were able to manoeuvre across the poor roads.

LEFT: After three months of continuous combat, Guderian's 2nd *Panzergruppe* – in effect, an armoured army – had penetrated deep into Russian territory. *Das Reich* had seen action for all but the first few days, and in September 1941 it was withdrawn for a short period of rest and recuperation, during which this officer has acquired a pair of puppies. Once back in the line, *Das Reich* was used in the vast battle of encirclement around Kiev in the Ukraine.

RIGHT: A *Das Reich* officer poses for the camera outside an Orthodox country church, in a photograph taken during the autumn of 1941. At this time, the division had already disengaged from the victorious encirclement of Kiev to drive north-wards again, tasked with breaking through the defensive positions guarding the Red capital. The *Barbarossa* campaign had already taken a toll on *Das Reich*. By September, the *Deutschland* Regiment alone had lost more than 1500 men killed, wounded or missing. The *Der Führer* Regiment and other units of the division had suffered similar losses.

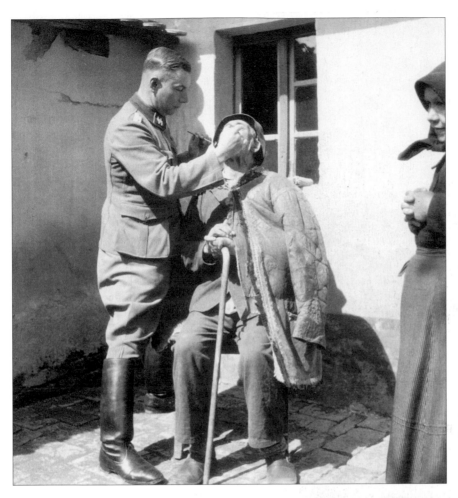

LEFT: An unusual photograph showing a *Das Reich* dentist preparing to extract a tooth from a local Polish peasant prior to the launch of *Barbarossa* in June 1941. Although many of the highly indoctrinated, even brainwashed *SS* troopers regarded the Poles and all Slavs as sub-humans, there were exceptions. Many *SS* soldiers treated locals cordially and courteously, and even provided malnourished residents with bread and soup. Even in Russia during pauses in fighting, some *SS* troops showed varying degrees of kindness to the locals. However, this must be balanced against the fanaticism which led the *SS* to commit frequent atrocities against civilians and prisoners of war.

RIGHT: The *Das Reich* dentist deals with another local patient, who appears to be in some degree of pain. Undoubtedly the procedure was being carried out without the benefit of anaesthetic. Within weeks, these troops would be embroiled in combat on the Eastern Front. Because Army Group Centre had not allocated the *SS* division any space in its early movement plans, *Das Reich* troopers had to march long distances by foot, hitching lifts where possible with the vehicles of the 2nd *Panzergruppe*. The division's initial task was to force a river crossing between Citva and Dukora, and for the mission it used a detachment comprising reconnaissance, motorcycle, flak and pioneer units. It moved along Highway 1, capturing the village of Starzyca and providing flank security to the northern edge of Guderian's drive along the main trunk road between Minsk and Smolensk.

ABOVE: *SS Polizei* troops with a captured Soviet 76.2mm (3in) Infantry Gun Model 1927 (76-27). The gun was used extensively by the Red Army on the Eastern Front and was a very successful weapon. It weighed only 780kg (1720lb) in action and fired a 6.21kg (13lb 11oz) shell to a maximum range of 8555m (9356yd). Massive numbers of these infantry guns were captured by the Germans and became so popular that German factories actually manufactured ammunition for them, fitting their own sights.

LEFT: Two *Das Reich* officers stand beside the road while awaiting a parade to march past. Both men are wearing fine quality officer's greatcoats. The army-style green-faced collar was standard early in the conflict, though as the war progressed the collar patches of service and rank were seen less and less frequently on greatcoats. The shoulder straps are sewn in at the shoulder seams. They are both wearing their greatcoats over army-style woollen tunics, and in this instance these are almost certainly privately tailored items of very high quality. Both of them are wearing the regulation *SS* officer's leather belt and aluminium buckle. The service dress cap is also of high quality, with aluminium cords and white cap piping. Collar patches and epaulettes were usually piped in different colours known as *Waffenfarbe*, which indicated the wearer's branch of service (armour, infantry, *et cetera*).

LEFT: *Das Reich* officers in contrasting dress styles. The *SS Untersturmführer* is in field dress, while his comrade wears an *SS* officer's Party Parade uniform. The *SS* had little of the class system so prevalent in the Prussian-dominated army. Officers stressed the comradeship of serving in a racial elite. Even in the midst of battle, *SS* commanders strove to lead their men by example, making sure that the special bond remained intact.

RIGHT: A *Das Reich* medic checks a local peasant child. Such friendly scenes were not the norm: as members of an elite formation, the *SS* men carried with them a sense of their superiority, which was heightened by the fact that they were encouraged to look on Eastern Europeans as sub-humans. This became the justification for any number of terrible atrocities. Even so, many Soviets, especially in areas like the Ukraine, regarded the Germans as their saviours from the oppression of Stalin and the communists. The *SS* even provided business for the local Russian tradesmen, who could mend boots and other personal equipment.

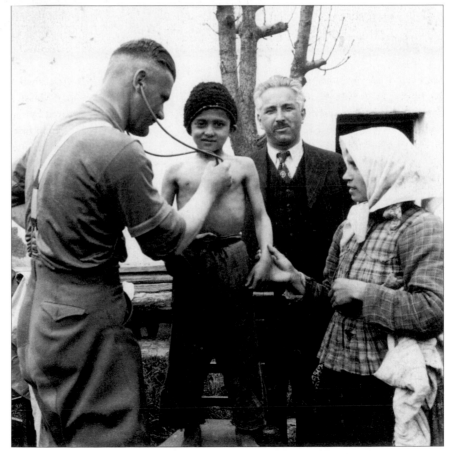

RIGHT: A *Das Reich* trooper inspects a destroyed Soviet warplane during the early phases of *Barbarossa*. At the time, the division numbered 19,021 troops, considerably more than an army division. It was not, however, the largest *SS* formation. The newly formed *Wiking* Division had 19,377 troops. The *Totenkopf* had 18,754 on strength, the *Polizei* numbered 17,347. *Leibstandarte* and *Nord*, both being expanded from brigade to divisional size, had 10,796, and 10,573 men respectively.

LEFT: A *Das Reich* soldier smiles for the camera with the two Russian puppies seen earlier. He is wearing an early first-pattern type smock worn green side outermost. He is also wearing the M1938 *Feldmütze* with death's head badge. Note the tactical symbol painted in yellow and the divisional insignia painted in white on the rear of the Horch vehicle. *Das Reich's* insignia was a rune that resembled a reversed 'N' with a vertical line running down the middle of it. It was know as the 'Wolfsangel', and it was an ancient symbol that was supposed to protect those that wore it from wolves.

**ABOVE:** A column of *Das Reich* vehicles seen during the division's drive towards Moscow. For now, the going is good, but in a matter of weeks, even days, these vehicles would be bogged down in the seemingly bottomless Russian mud. From the first days of *Barbarossa*, German soldiers soon realized the immensity of their task. Roads were few, and cross-country travel caused its own problems. In dry weather, vehicles had to use unmetalled roads, little more than tracks, and the sand and dust kicked up by continuous traffic frequently ruined engines and other vital mechanical parts. In spring and autumn – the rainy seasons – mud was everywhere, and even those vehicles which avoided being bogged down had air intakes and exhausts plugged. Coupled with the sheer size of the country, the Russian weather offered the invaders considerably greater challenges than they had faced in Poland and in Western Europe.

**RIGHT:** A group of *Das Reich* officers pause in their drive east to confer in what little high ground the Russian flat lands offered. Note the Horch vehicle with *Das Reich*'s identifying letter 'G' painted in white on the rear. As one would expect, the licence plate carries *SS* markings. *Das Reich* fought hard in Russia, but at some cost. The high rate of loss experienced by the division in the first month of combat accelerated in July and early August, when it fought a number of brutal battles. In particular, *Das Reich* saw such stiff action around the town of Yelnya that its infantry losses forced General Guderian to relieve the division, sending it back to rest and replacing it with *Wehrmacht* units, which were also to suffer severe casualties at the hands of the determined Red Army.

LEFT: *Das Reich* soldiers prepare to be transported from Salzburg through Poland in June 1941. The division had been refitting in Austria after the campaign in the Balkans. En route from Austria, the troops were not told of their coming mission. These men were destined to play a major role in the war in Russia. As shock troops with deep-seated ideological and racial beliefs, they were willing to do whatever it took to destroy what they saw as the evil of Bolshevism, in the name of their beloved *Führer*.

BELOW: *Das Reich* is inspected by the divisional commander, *SS Obergruppenführer* Paul Hausser. 'Papa' Hausser was a key player in the development of the *Waffen-SS*. Following the campaign in Poland, Hausser organized the *Deutschland*, *Germania* and *Der Führer* Regiments into the *SS-Verfügungstruppe* Division, the *SS-VT*, which would eventually become known to friend and foe alike as *Das Reich*.

BELOW RIGHT: *Das Reich* on parade. In September, following the great victory at Kiev, optimism was high. The troops were certain that they would reach Moscow within weeks – in front of Army Group Centre stood the weakest Soviet army yet encountered. These Soviet forces would soon be subjected to the kind of all-out assault which had given Germany such triumphs in the first two years of battle.

RIGHT: Two *Waffen-SS* soldiers teach Ukrainian volunteers how to use a mortar. The Ukraine had suffered dreadfully under Stalin in the 1930s, when millions had died in famines. The Ukrainian peasants welcomed the Germans as liberators, but Germany's attitude towards the Ukraine was complex and contradictory. At first, the army appreciated the fervent Ukrainian appreciation for liberation, and two battalions of Ukrainian nationalists were raised by the *Abwehr* to serve as commando units behind the Soviet Army lines. However, the Nazi provincial administration, which was established after the conquest, behaved with the utmost cruelty and brutality towards a population it saw as nothing but *Untermenschen,* By 1943, Himmler decided that western Ukraine – ancient Galicia – was sufficiently 'Aryan' to allow its men to enter the *SS*. 'Galicians' volunteered for the *Waffen-SS* in some numbers, not only to keep the Soviet Army

out but to gain access to the military training and equipment essential to win their freedom from either (or both) totalitarian systems.

ABOVE: An MG 34 machine gunner moves forward under the protection of a StuG.III assault gun of the SS-*Totenkopf* Division. This vehicle is armed with a 7.5cm (2.95in) StuK 37 L/24 gun. Note the *Totenkopf* insignia – painted in red with a black background – on the front of the assault gun. In reserve when 'Barbarossa' was unleashed, the *Totenkopf* rolled across the East Prussian border on 24/25 June. Attached to *Generalfeldmarschall* Ritter von Leeb's Army Group North, the Division served with Erich Hoeppner's 4th Panzer Group. After clearing the Lithuanian forests around Jurbarkas, *Totenkopf* moved towards the Dvina, where on 27 June it made its first real contact with Soviet forces.

**ABOVE:** *Das Reich* troops march past a dead Russian soldier sprawled out across a forest track. In the campaign fought in western Russia, terrain was an important factor. The *SS* soon found that the Baltic republics and the adjoining Russian territory were heavily forested. Woodland fighting calls for its own special skills – skills which had largely been over-looked in both *Waffen-SS* and *Wehrmacht* invasion manuals. Even woodsmen brought up in places like the Black Forest had never experienced anything like the great expanses of trees set in tangled undergrowth so dense that movement was almost impossible. Some parts of these forests were in a primeval state, seemingly unvisited by man. German troops who fought in these forested regions seldom penetrated very deeply while on patrol, partly due to the difficulty of movement but also for fear of ambush. The forest provided natural hiding places for the growing bands of Soviet partisans, and the Germans were never able to clear the woods of their enemies completely.

**LEFT:** Two soldiers of the *Polizei* Division pose for the camera in front of a batch of Soviet prisoners. By the end of September, it was estimated by the Germans that the Soviets had lost at least two and a half million men killed or taken prisoner, and that 22,000 guns, 18,000 tanks and 14,000 aircraft had been destroyed. The victory at Kiev had encouraged Hitler and some of the General Staff that one final push would capture Moscow and finish the Red Army off. Yet in spite of these whirlwind gains, many ordinary soldiers felt uncomfortable, deep in an alien land whose people simply would not lie down and die.

ABOVE: A StuG.III Ausf. B belonging to the *Totenkopf* Division has lost a track during operations in late November 1941. The assault gun has been given a camouflage paint of whitewash. By now, the great German offensive all along the Eastern Front was grinding to a halt. The *Totenkopf* and the rest of the

16th Army began to dig in for the harsh winter ahead. During November, German supply lines became increasingly overstretched and casualty returns were mounting ominously. The *Totenkopf* was no exception, and its already high losses began to grow as disease and frostbite began to take hold.

LEFT: A pair of *Waffen-SS* Pz.Kpfw.IIIs ready to resume their advance. The aims of the German armoured spearhead in Russia had been very ambitious. The *Wehrmacht* was, in fact, attempting too much: Germany simply did not have either enough men or equipment to support three simultaneous thrusts into Russia. The Panzers had only limited cross-country endurance, in a land which called for operations across vast distances. Virtually all of their supply vehicles were wheeled, which tied them to the roads. According to the maps, a number of the roads were suitable for a mechanized advance, but this was soon found to be an illusion. Tank crews found themselves inching forward along either dusty or boggy tracks, depending on the season, and the movement of the wheeled vehicles on which they relied for support was almost impossible.

BELOW: A StuG.III Ausf. B carrying the *Totenkopf* unit emblem prominently displayed on the front plate beside the gun. The emblem was normally painted a different colour in each battery, red in the first battery, yellow in the second battery and green in the third battery, all in a black rectangle. As in this photograph, they used a two-digit tactical number system on later version StuG.IIIs, which was painted in white above the unit emblem. Track links attached to the front of the vehicle provide extra protection.

BELOW: *Totenkopf* troops supported by a StuG.III assault gun move through the town of Opochka. In early July 1941, the *SS-Totenkopf* Division was assigned to Manstein's 56th Panzer Corps, part of Army Group North. The division was given the task of guarding the corps flank while maintaining contact with the 16th Army to the south. On 5 July, the *Totenkopf* was the spearhead of the corps' attack on the heavily fortified Stalin Line, along with the 56th Panzer Corps. The *SS* men were surprised at the dense fortifications. Losses were high for the Soviets, who were determined not to lose the key town of Opochka.

RIGHT: *Totenkopf* flamethrower troops in action against a heavily defended Soviet position, probably in early July along the Stalin Line south of Leningrad. This consisted of a strongly defended string of bunkers, wire and minefields. By this time, the Red Army was recovering after the initial shock of the German invasion. Although the men of the *Totenkopf* were able to drive off the initial counter-attacks without much difficulty, they were gradually being worn down by repeated frontal assaults. In some areas, Soviet soldiers fought to the death rather than surrender to the Germans.

LEFT: Pz.Kpfw.III Ausf. J tanks accompanied by *SS* infantrymen move across the open steppe in August 1941. The Panzer III was the standard medium tank of the *Panzer* divisions at this time, and equipped the *Panzer* battalions that the *SS* had added to the motorized divisions *Das Reich* and *Wiking*. Early examples of this variant were equipped with the 5cm (1.96in) KwK L/42 gun. Subsequent *Panzers* mounted the much more lethal long-barrelled 5cm KwK 39 L/60 gun, although it was still no match for the 76mm (3in) gun mounted by the Soviet T-34. Note the soldier armed with the anti-tank mine. This had a large explosive charge that could easily disable a tank by damaging a track or wheel. The most common mine used by the *Waffen-SS* was the Teller-Mine.

# WINTER WAR

**The German advance on Moscow was the first time *Wehrmacht* and *Waffen-SS* troops were to experience the harsh realities of winter on the Eastern Front.**

It was on 6 October 1941 that the weather began to change, as cold driving rain fell on Army Group Centre's front. Soon the rain turned into snow and the German advance gradually ground to a halt in front of Moscow. Day after day, the ingredients of disaster were building as the German offensive burned itself out. In early December, the situation worsened as the temperature dropped. Many soldiers were reluctant to emerge from their shelter to fight during the blizzards. Hundreds of tanks were abandoned in the drifting snow, and the crews retreated. Despair gripped the frozen German front lines. Slowly the entire central front began to disintegrate in the snow, isolated and with unusable vehicles, small arms frozen solid, the actions of machine guns seized up in the cold temperatures which

LEFT: *SS-Totenkopf* men shuffle across the snow on the Leningrad Front. To the south, their comrades in Army Group Centre were near to collapse. By early December 1941, the situation had become critical as the temperature dropped. A soldier noted in his diary: 'Here in this endless expanse of Russia the snow is burying every object in its path. We slog forward hour after hour half-starved in our insufficient clothing... We are slowly freezing to death.'

35

reached as low as -40°C (-40°F). But forcing a way through the blizzards, an exhausted *Das Reich* reconnaissance battalion managed to reach the Moscow city tramcar system terminus on 4 December 1941. But this was the farthest point reached in the assault.

All over the central front, battered and frostbitten forces ground to a halt in the arctic conditions. Then, on 5 December, the Soviets launched a counteroffensive with fresh troops drawn from the far east. The German army collapsed, and a massive defeat loomed.

Hitler would have none of this. Haunted by the spectre of Napoleon's retreat from Moscow, he would not allow the *Wehrmacht* to turn its back, even momentarily, on the Russian capital. 'Where would they retreat to?' he asked. 'Is it warmer 50 km or 100 km to the west?'

There would be no retreat. The German army would stand fast, just as it had in World War I. Any generals who protested were sacked.

Hitler's iron will held the troops in place, but at enormous cost. German losses to the end of December 1941 were massive. They had lost 500,000 men, 1300 tanks, 2500 guns and more than 1600 vehicles. The *Das Reich* Division, for instance, lost 60 per cent of its fighting strength, all because of its allegiance to the *Führer,* and its willingness to obey him to the letter. Along the front, the soldiers held their ground in appalling conditions. There was not enough food; intense cold and inadequate shelter increased the misery. The army reported over 100,000 frostbite cases in December alone. Indeed, frostbite caused more hospitalization than Soviet guns. Hypothermia would soon be killing more.

On the Leningrad front, conditions for the *Totenkopf* Division were no better. It had battled its way through snow blizzards in the region of Demyansk, and it was here that the Red Army launched a massive counteroffensive during the night of 7–8 January 1942. Within a few days, the situation for the *Totenkopf* became critical as they were squeezed into the Demyansk pocket. By 8 February, some 95,000 *Wehrmacht* and *Waffen-SS* troops, together with 20,000 horses, were trapped in the pocket. As the situation worsened, Hitler repeated his 'no withdrawal' orders, saying that every soldier must hold his position until a new front could be established, from where a relief attack could be unleashed. Throughout February and early March, the *Totenkopf* men were subjected to constant Soviet aerial and ground bombardment. The troops fought on in chest-deep snow. Although by early March the division was on the verge of destruction, it continued its fanatical resistance until the spring thaws eventually arrived in mid-March.

The first winter on the Eastern Front had been a complete misery for both *Wehrmacht*

---

**For the first time, the myth of the invincibility of the German army had been broken. Though few knew it at the time, the defeat at the gates of Moscow signalled the beginning of the end for the 'Thousand Year Reich'.**

---

and *Waffen-SS* troops. None of the soldiers had expected to be fighting the war against the Soviet Union into the winter of 1941. Life on the Eastern Front became a battle for survival, even for the most committed of *SS* soldiers. Despondency spread throughout the ranks, but with the winter finally mastered they believed that victory would soon be theirs. However, by mid-1942 it became apparent that there would be no victory that year.

With the prospect of fighting another winter war, the *Wehrmacht* quickly produced a handbook on winter warfare. This asserted that all soldiers could meet and overcome the terrors of living and fighting in subzero temperatures. Much of the book concerned itself with ways in which to overcome the appallingly cold Russian winter. Whole chapters dealt with constructing shelters. Other chapters were devoted to the subjects of clothing, food, animal care, vehicle camouflage

ABOVE: Troops of the 6th *SS-Gebirgs* Division on patrol. Originally known as *Kampfgruppe Nord*, the unit was upgraded to divisional status in June 1941. Mountain and arctic warfare specialists, the division served in the far north until November 1944, when it was transferred to the West. These ski troopers are wearing heavy padded reversible clothing. The jacket allows access to the uniform underneath via the pockets. The white padded mittens were specially designed with a 'finger' to allow weapons to be fired.

and the way in which tank track marks could be concealed in the snow. The manual outlined the construction of primitive but effective stoves and pointed out the best ways of avoiding carbon monoxide poisoning.

Throughout the book, great efforts were made to convince the German soldier that the snow could also serve as an ally. It stressed that snow was wind-resistant and could act as a shelter and as a windshield to protect engines of vehicles parked in the open.

The winter warfare handbook was a well-researched piece of literature that undoubtedly helped the German soldier resolve many of the problems of fighting in a Russian winter. But it came too late to save those who had died in 1941.

Most of the German army was woefully unprepared for the arctic conditions – though some *Waffen-SS* units had made preparations.

During their advance, a number of well-organized weatherproof dumps had been set up, consisting of food and fuel supplies, ammunition and warm clothing. Not all clothing suitable for a Russian winter war had reached the front during that first winter, but by the following year adequate supplies of reversible, quilted jackets, trousers, special fur caps and white camouflage smocks had been distributed extensively to the men.

Although the winter clothing issued to the *SS* in 1942 was basically the same as that used by the *Wehrmacht*, by 1943 the *Waffen-SS* were issued with new winter clothing that was reversible from *SS* pattern camouflage to white.

But despite the various forms of protective clothing issued to the troops, especially after the terrible winter of 1941, both the *Wehrmacht* and *Waffen-SS* continued to suffer during the remaining two Russian winters. Abnormally low temperatures not only killed many thousands of men through frostbite and disease, but also led to an indelible breakdown in military cohesion and unit efficiency.

LEFT: Red Army prisoners digging trenches for the Germans during the drive on Moscow in November 1941. Note that they are still dressed in their summer uniforms. The *Das Reich* guards are also not very suitably dressed; they are wearing standard army issue greatcoats. There had been little preparation made at the high levels of command to outfit German soldiers with the appropriate clothing, weapons and food to withstand the horrors of a Russian winter. Snow fell as early as the first week of October, and the severe temperatures made it almost impossible for those men who were not adequately protected to remain outside.

RIGHT: Horses tow supply sleds for *Das Reich*. Note the large amount of hay being carried; as much as 40 percent of the total tonnage of supplies used by horse-drawn units was devoted to fodder. Horses still played a major part in the German logistics effort in 1942, but they suffered even more than the men. Many were killed by aerial machine-gunning, shellfire and heart failure, brought on by exertion. Horses also died of the cold, for they were less resilient than humans. Men in proper clothing could remain alive out in the open for a whole night at subzero temperatures, but horses protected only by their own hides died if they were exposed for the same length of time to cold temperatures.

ABOVE: *Das Reich* vehicles halt on the main highway to Moscow in November 1941. Note two of the soldiers wearing Soviet-style felt over boots, which were much more effective at insulating feet than the standard German jackboot. The *Waffen-SS* would learn from the winter of 1941 and would overcome many of the problems of winter wear the following year. But it was at great cost. Although this road has been cleared of snow, vehicles would be immobilized within a month by deep drifts. Supply trucks would be unable to reach the fighting units, leading to chronic shortages of ammunition, fuel and food.

RIGHT: Two *Das Reich* signallers in action during the battle for Moscow late in November 1941. *Das Reich* had joined Operation *Typhoon* on the morning of 4 October, when the division attacked towards the towns of Krichev and Ladishino with units of the 10th *Panzer* Division. By mid-October, when the first snow showers cast their deadly spell on the Eastern Front, the men of *Das Reich* were heavily embroiled in a full-scale attack upon the outer defences of Moscow. Spearheading the assault were battalions of the *Der Führer* Regiment. At the same time, north of the Moscow highway, the *Deutschland* Regiment found itself in an intense battle with two fresh Mongolian infantry battalions.

ABOVE: Troops of the 6th *SS-Gebirgs* Division *Nord* seen during an operation in Army Group North. *Nord* saw more action than almost any other German unit, fighting for 1214 consecutive days in the sub-arctic taiga against the Soviets, from 1 July 1941 through to the autumn of 1944. All are wearing the shapeless two-piece snowsuit consisting of a white jacket and white trousers. With Red Army forces wearing similar clothing, front line German troops were issued with coloured arm bands for use on their winter clothing. These enabled them to distinguish between friend and foe. Note that all their weapons, including Kar 98K bolt-action rifles and MP 40 sub-machine guns, have received a winter coat of whitewash.

ABOVE: A column of 6th *SS-Gebirgs* ski troops advance across frozen Russian terrain accompanied by horse-drawn sledges. Fighting against the Red Army during the winter of 1941 was fierce, since the Soviets were in their element. The division suffered heavy casualties in the combined German/Finnish attempt to cut the Soviet rail line to Murmansk. It was the last major offensive in the region, combat settling down to static operations along the Kiestinki–Louhi road.

RIGHT: The *SS* mountain division was originally formed in Norway early in 1941, with men from *SS-Totenkopfstandarten* 6 and 7, to which were added the *Nachrichtenabteilung* from the *SS-Verfügungsdivision*. Later it became a division, incorporating a mixture of both German and ethnic German personnel. In 1943, Norwegian collaborationist ski troopers were attached to the division, eventually forming an elite *Waffen-SS Schijäger* battalion.

ABOVE: A *Totenkopf* soldier halts his dogsled in the snow during a lull in the fighting early in January 1942. By 12 January, the situation in Army Group North had become critical. Field Marshal Ritter von Leeb believed that the only course of action was to withdraw over the River Lovat and form a strong defensive line. When Leeb requested permission to withdraw, Hitler refused outright, and ordered the soldiers to stand fast. As a consequence of Hitler's orders, two German corps were squeezed into a pocket at Demyansk as Red Army formations counterattacked and broke through along the River Lovat.

ABOVE: A group of *Totenkopf* men advance through the night during a desperate battle near Staraya. This photograph was taken early in January 1942 after the Soviets had unleashed an offensive against Army Group North's southern flank. It was here that Soviet units smashed into the *Totenkopf* and its neighbours, the 30th and 290th Infantry Divisions. The front quickly collapsed, with the 290th Infantry Division bearing the brunt of the Soviet fury. On 9 January, a number of *Totenkopf* units were sent in to stiffen the front against collapse. What followed was a bitter and bloody battle of attrition in the snow.

LEFT: Ski troops of the *SS* Division *Nord* seen during a reconnaissance mission early in 1942. Skis were a very effective means of movement across frozen terrain, and were used extensively by reconnaissance patrols. The division initially fought poorly, but after training with Finnish troops in the autumn of 1941 it became a highly effective unit, often serving alongside the Army's 7th *Gebirgsjäger* Division.

ABOVE: *Totenkopf* soldiers in action in the Demyansk Pocket in February 1942. An MG 34 machine gun has been set up on a sustained fire mount and the gunner and feeder can be seen poised to use this potent weapon in anger. Hitler's order to stand and fight to the death was the kind of instruction that these hard-bitten soldiers of the *SS* understood best. Unlike their *Wehrmacht* counterparts, the *Totenkopf* were well suited to winter warfare, having been provided with ample supplies of winter clothing.

LEFT: *Totenkopf* ski troops take up positions during fighting in the Demyansk Pocket. Although the skill and tenacity of these *SS* soldiers prevented a total rout in northern Russia, the division's success was bought at an appalling cost in men and materiel. At one point, divisional strength, which had been around 18,000 men in June 1941, fell to just 51 officers and 2685 men. In August 1942 Hitler decreed that the unit should be rebuilt as a *Panzergrenadier* division.

ABOVE: A long column of *Totenkopf* troops hauling their supplies through the snow using horse and sled. This picture was taken during a lull in the months of fighting in the Demyansk Pocket. Movement was very risky during daylight hours, as Red Army aircraft regularly attacked German formations out in the open. They also dropped thousands of incendiary bombs on buildings to deny any form of shelter to the *Totenkopf*, who were fighting in subzero temperatures in waist-high snow.

RIGHT: A *Totenkopf* MG 34 gunner somewhere inside the Demyansk Pocket in February 1942. As the Soviets closed the ring around Demyansk, the *Totenkopf* troops trapped inside were split into two *Kampfgruppen*, which included army personnel. Theodor Eicke, who was ordered to defend the southwest sector of the pocket, commanded the first *Kampfgruppe*. On the northwest edge of the pocket, *SS Oberführer* Max Simon commanded the second *Kampfgruppe*.

ABOVE: A *Totenkopf* mortar crew about to fire a shell during defensive combat in the Demyansk Pocket. Note the number of discarded ammunition boxes, indicating the degree of fighting raging in the area. In spite of the Red Army increasing the scale and intensity of their infantry and armoured attacks, the *Waffen-SS* held onto their positions in the name of the *Führer*. In almost every area on the edge of the pocket, the *Totenkopf* were outnumbered by the Soviets, but these *SS* men were masters in defence and continued resisting, beating off constant enemy attacks. *Totenkopf*, along with major units of the 18th Army, was trapped in the pocket from January to 14 April 1942, when a three-mile corridor was punched through to the besieged troops. Elements of the division remained at Demyansk until October 1942.

RIGHT: A *Totenkopf* soldier seen during operations inside the Demyansk Pocket in February 1942. This *SS* man has been kitted out with ample winter clothing. The *Totenkopf* Division had received a large shipment of winter gear just before the pocket was closed, delivered from the massive SS supply dump established at Riga, in the Baltic state of Latvia. Most of the clothing was looted from the estates of Jews executed by *SS-Einsatzgruppen* or by their willing Latvian assistants. However, while the men appreciated the protection from the cold, they soon started complaining. The clothing was too bulky, which reduced the wearer's mobility and also restricted visibility. The headpiece worn by this particular soldier was designed to help contain as much body heat as possible and to prevent discomfort from the arctic temperatures whilst wearing the standard issue steel helmet. Troops often complained that the helmets were like 'freezer boxes' during the winter. Heat loss through the head lowered their body temperatures. This led to the very real dangers of exposure as well as poten-tially fatal cases of hypothermia.

LEFT: A 6th *SS-Gebirgs* soldier leads a dogsled. He is camouflaged in the standard two-piece snow-suit, and carries a white-painted snow-camouflaged rifle. The snowsuit's jacket is buttoned right down the front with white painted buttons and has an attached white hood. The white trousers were worn over the winter clothing and were tucked into the boots. Note the coloured armband worn on the soldier's arm as an identification sign. Its colour or position was usually altered according to a frequently changing security sequence.

RIGHT: A *Totenkopf* MG 34 machine gun crew in a defensive position on the edge of the Demyansk Pocket. The machine gun has been attached to a *Lafette* 34 sustained-fire mount. The gunner uses a grip trigger that has a mechanical linkage to the trigger on the gun. The MG 34 had tremendous staying power on the battlefield, as long as the machine gun crew could keep their weapon fully operational and deployed with good fields of fire. In the Demyansk Pocket, as elsewhere, well-placed machine gun crews managed to hold up entire attacking regiments for hours at a time.

ABOVE: Two 6th *SS-Gebirgs* troops are on the lookout for the next Soviet attack. The rifleman is armed with a captured Soviet SVT-40 Tokarev self-loading rifle. These were popular trophies with both German and Finnish troops, as they were accurate and their semi-automatic action gave them a much higher rate of fire than the standard German issue bolt-action Mauser. Other popular captured weapons included the PPSh-41 sub-machine gun, which was much more reliable than the MP 40 in the harsh Russian winter.

RIGHT: Several *Waffen-SS* and *Wehrmacht* units built igloos to shelter from the arctic winds, and to use as machine gun nests. In this photo-graph, a *Totenkopf* MG 34 gunner can be seen preparing to fire his potent weapon. Note the ammunition box with a 50-round belt of bullets. The MG 34 could fire at a cyclic rate of 900 rounds per minute, but experienced gunners usually limited their fire to 3-to-5 round bursts.

LEFT: A Tokarev-armed ski trooper attached to the 6th *SS-Gebirgs* Division on reconnaissance near the enemy lines in February 1942. Note that the trooper's binoculars are protected by a white knitted woollen cover. This was done not only to camouflage the binoculars, but also to protect the relatively fragile working parts from the extreme cold of the arctic conditions. Despite the terrors of the Russian winter, during which the Red Army had a considerable advantage, the Germans were determined not to be beaten. Instead of retreating across the drifting snowfields, with the possibility of being cut to pieces by the enemy, both *Wehrmacht* and *Waffen-SS* men dug in and fought it out, waiting for the spring thaw to arrive.

ABOVE: A group of ski troopers of the 6th *SS* Division *Nord* in February 1942. The soldiers are armed with a mix of weapons, including Kar 98K bolt-action rifles, MP 40 sub-machine guns and a captured Tokarev. Sub-machine guns were used extensively by *SS* ski troops and by their Soviet counterparts. They offered less of a burden than rifles while skiing, and they could be brought into action much more quickly. The MP 40 had an effective range of 200m (220yd), although practical ranges were usually less than half that, and could fire 9mm (0.35in) rounds at cyclic rates of up to 500 rounds per minute. It used a 32-round magazine.

RIGHT: *Totenkopf* troops belonging to Eicke's *Kampfgruppe* patrol the edge of the Demyansk Pocket on horseback. A village in the background can be seen coming under heavy attack. This was a desperate battle of attrition, but Eicke firmly believed that his men were superior and that their resistance would wear down the Soviet onslaught. His men did indeed fight with skill and endurance, but he drove them to the ends of that endurance.

ABOVE: During a lull in the Demyansk fighting, a *Totenkopf* mortar crew takes time out to have a much needed cigarette. They are all wearing the two-piece snowsuit and their steel helmets have received an application of whitewash for camouflage. Through February and early March 1942, the *Totenkopf* was under continuous pressure, yet in most sectors of the front they did not retreat from their positions in temperatures that averaged 30°C below zero (-22°F). This photograph was taken in late February. It would not be until 21 March that a serious attempt was made to relieve the pocket.

ABOVE: A photograph showing *Totenkopf* troops on the move in late February 1942. These soldiers appear to be dispersed following a heavy enemy attack. To the rear, a village is on fire, probably caused by incendiary bombs dropped by the Soviet air force. The battle of the pocket reached its climax at the end of February, when strong Soviet forces directed the bulk of its troops against Eicke's western part of the western sector. The Soviet onslaught at times was so vicious that it cut Eicke's command into isolated individual pockets, but the determined men of the *Waffen-SS* continued to hold out at terrible cost.

LEFT: *SS-Totenkopf* soldiers on their way to the front lines in the Demyansk Pocket. The Red Army could field some 15 fresh infantry divisions against the exhausted German forces. With the pocket becoming increasingly constricted, the *Luftwaffe* successfully began supplying the beleaguered troops by air with an estimated 200 tonnes daily. Some supplies were flown in directly to an improvized airfield in the pocket, from where sick and wounded could be evacuated, while others were dropped by parachute. This was the first time that an operation of this scale had ever been attempted. In the opinion of the *Wehrmacht*, the air supply operations were decisive in enabling the encircled forces to hold out.

ABOVE: The temperatures on the Eastern Front needed to be experienced to be believed. It was imperative that every soldier wrapped up warm to prevent both hypothermia and frostbite. Soldiers had to acclimatize quickly to these arctic conditions. Those that did not, died. Although these troops may be relatively well equipped with winter clothing, each man knew he was fighting the cold alone, pitting morale, courage and determination to live against the bitterest winter in a century of bitter winters. The physical strain of ploughing through waist-deep snow, added to the cold and the prospect of combat without pause, exhausted the men to the point where they became easy victims of respiratory diseases. Under the cumulative effects of strain, of sickness and of battle casualties, front-line formations were quickly reduced to groups of worn out and badly depleted men who were unable to sustain themselves on the battlefield.

LEFT: Ski troops of the 6th *SS-Gebirgs* Division consult a map during a reconnaissance patrol. The whole area in the extreme northern part of the Eastern Front was poor in west-east communications, and the Soviet defenders of the key port of Murmansk depended on a single main road and rail link from Leningrad and Moscow. German and Finnish mountain troops made one determined effort to cut the link, attacking out of northern Norway and Finland. However, once the attack had been beaten off, the war in the area settled down to a static conflict of continual patrols and raiding. Map-reading was a vital skill in crossing bleak and featureless expanses of tundra, or in moving through seemingly endless forests.

LEFT: Injured *Totenkopf* troops rejoining their comrades after receiving basic first aid. Only the most seriously wounded had any chance of being evacuated by air. In the desperate battle in the Demyansk Pocket, the men of the *SS* were increasingly weakened by privation and exertion, terrified by the hostility of the arctic weather and by continuous Red Army attacks. Each *SS* man knew that he existed in a desert of snow and ice, but within its desolation he had, as one soldier later wrote: 'our songs and our spirit'.

RIGHT: *Totenkopf* troops seen early in March 1942. These ski troops were particularly effective against enemy formations, appearing suddenly out of the snow to sweep across a trench line, spraying bullets from machine pistols and hurling grenades before disappearing into the concealing snow clouds. By this period of the battle, illness and injury meant that there were fewer and fewer soldiers available to hold the line. A relief attempt was now only weeks away, but it would come at a great cost to this most fanatical of all the elite *Waffen-SS* divisions.

ABOVE: *Totenkopf* soldiers prepare to move off along another battle line in the Demyansk Pocket. This photograph was taken west of the Lovat river. For weeks, the *Totenkopf* were employed in the most hard-pressed areas of the pocket. Its two *Kampfgruppen* were used as 'fire brigade' units, plugging gaps wherever they appeared in the front. The German counterattack to relieve the pocket was finally unleashed on 21 March, but stiff Red Army resistance meant that the German advance, under the command of Lieutenant General Walter von Seydlitz, temporarily stalled, and it did not break through until 14 April.

RIGHT: An MG 34 machine gun position. The machine gun is mounted on the MG-*Lafette* 34 sustained-fire mount. Note the optical sight. The MG 34 was 1219mm (48in) long and weighed 31.07kg (68lb 8oz) on the sustained-fire mount. With a muzzle velocity of 755m (2477ft) a second, it had a maximum range of 2000m (2187yd) and a cyclic firing rate of 800-900 rounds per minute. The *Waffen-SS* used the MG 34 and the later MG 42 extensively on the Eastern Front.

LEFT: Life in the line for *SS-Totenkopf* soldiers in the Demyansk pocket was a continuous grind of guard duty and patrols. To be able to sleep for more than three hours uninterrupted seemed a rare luxury. There was little respite – if the Soviets ever let up for a brief period, the winter certainly did not. On the edge of the pocket, life was very difficult. Numb and cold, in spite of their winter clothing, they would stumble back into their shelters – primitive dugouts, whose air was thick with choking smoke. By March 1942, most of the men were infested with lice, and to make matters worse they could not undress in the cold dugout to pick off and kill the vermin.

LEFT: 6th *SS-Gebirgs* soldiers build an igloo for shelter. Under extreme arctic conditions, it was vital to bring every man under cover at night, and guard duty was limited to short periods. The igloos the men built had a number of advantages – being made of snow, they were naturally camouflaged, and their thick walls were wind-proof and provided insulation against the cold. Their occupants lay close to one another to keep warm. The strongest men frequently gave up the chance of lying down in favour of weaker or wounded comrades.

RIGHT: A well wrapped-up *Waffen-SS* soldier in white camouflage smock. The *SS*, along with their *Wehrmacht* counterparts, made many great sacrifices during the winter of 1941–42. Those that managed to survive the ordeal got a medal to prove they had been there. Troops nicknamed this decoration the 'Frozen Meat Medal', as many of them had experienced uncovering the frozen corpses of their dead comrades and giving them proper burials. The period of qualification for the winter medal was from 15 November 1941 to 15 April 1942.

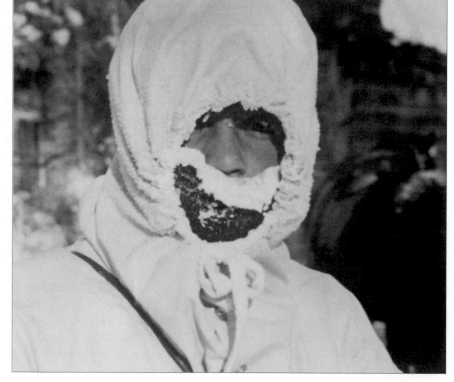

ABOVE: *Totenkopf* troops wearily make their way across the snow. The ground was normally too hard to dig, and most of the buildings had been destroyed in the fighting or burned by incendiary bombs. The extreme temperatures meant that virtually all the men on the front lines were unable to change their under-clothes – stripping off to do so invited frostbite or exposure. Those who sought more clothes undressed corpses after they had been killed. They had to act quickly, for once a body froze, it became impossible to strip off the uniform. On some parts of the front, the daytime temperatures remained at 40°C below zero (-40°F). The cold was so bad that rifle bolts froze, tanks and trucks would not start because their battery plates were warped, oil froze solid in the engine, cylinder blocks cracked, and axles refused to turn.

ABOVE: When the weather was at its most severe, there were very few men who could stand being unprotected on the frozen tundra for long. When the blizzards came, men were forced to dig in to protect themselves. Although cold, bare and miserable, these dugouts represented a sort of warmth, a protection from the wind, and a kind of makeshift home. Here the soldiers had to defend their own little kingdoms, fighting with almost lunatic desperation. To be driven from these dugouts meant that they might have to retreat, risking frostbite, hypothermia and almost certain death out in the open.

ABOVE: During the winter of 1941–42, the *Waffen-SS*, which was still less than 100,000 strong, had suffered massive casualties, losing over 8000 dead and 28,000 wounded. The harsh winter, the worst in a century, had in fact nearly cost the German army the war in the East. They had lost some 60 towns, and in some areas German troops had been pushed back 320km (200 miles). In spite of the terrors and casualties of the Russian winter, the *Waffen-SS* performance did not go unnoticed. They had stubbornly clung onto every yard of terrain with vigour and determination. Constantly they ran a gauntlet against heavy enemy fire, rushing from one position to another, filling gaps wrenched open by the Soviet onslaught. In a number of areas, the men, who were often fighting through bitterly cold weather against numerically superior forces, held on to the grim death, knowing that anything less would be disloyal to the *Führer*.

**ABOVE:** A *Totenkopf* mortar crew in action in the Demyansk Pocket. The mortar was used extensively by the premier *Waffen-SS* divisions, as it was with all German formations. It was light, easy to carry, and gave the infantryman his own portable light artillery support. But it required training to use; even experienced mortar crews could take several bombs to achieve just one successful hit on a target. The SS had three different mortar types, including the 8cm (3.6in) *Granatwerfer* 34 (8cm GW 34), which fired a 3.4kg (7lb 8oz) bomb to a maximum distance of 2400m (2626yd). There was also the 5cm (1.96in) *leichte Granatwerfer* 36 (leGW 36), which fired a small 0.9kg (1lb 15oz) bomb to a maximum range of only 500m (547yd). The largest mortar in operational service in the *Waffen-SS* was the 12cm *schwere Granatwerfer* 42 (sGW 42). The 12cm (4.7in) sGW 42 fired a 15.8kg (34lb 13oz) bomb to a range of 6050m (6619yd).

# EXPANSION OF THE *WAFFEN-SS*

In 1940, the *SS* still depended on native Germans for its recruitment. However, as the German forces overran much of Europe, the *Waffen-SS* began to expand, solving its manpower problems by enlisting ethnic Germans as well as suitably 'Nordic' volunteers.

*SS-Reichsführer* Heinrich Himmler became very interested in the recruitment of Germanic volunteers when he sought to expand the *Waffen-SS*. He wrote, 'we must attract all the Nordic blood in the world to us, and so deprive our enemies of it, so that never again will Nordic or Germanic blood fight against us.' In 1941, on the eve of the attack on the Soviet Union, Himmler speeded up the recruitment programme. The volunteers were often anti-communist to begin with, but they were led to believe that they were taking part in a kind of mystic Nordic crusade, the struggle of West against East for the sake of Western civilization.

The *SS* volunteer legions that joined the attack on Russia in 1941 consisted of some 400

LEFT: Inspection of a parade of foreign volunteers. During the course of the war, the *Waffen-SS*, which was intended as the cradle of the new Aryan superman, gradually evolved into a kind of German foreign legion, incorporating volunteers from all over Europe.

or so Flemings in the *Freiwilligen Legion Flandern*, the *Freikorps Danmark* comprising around 1000 Danish volunteers, the *Freiwilligen Legion Norwegen* manned by Norwegian *SS* recruits, and the *Finnische Freiwilligen-Bataillon der Waffen-SS*, which was eventually attached to the elite 5th *Wiking* Division. The last group of volunteers, which included *Volksdeutscher* 'ethnic German' recruits from Hungary and Romania together with a few Norwegians, formed the 6th *SS-Division Nord*, which was later to become a mountain division.

In 1942, the *Waffen-SS* not only saw further expansion of its foreign legions, but also saw reorganization within its own Germanic ranks. Units became fully motorized with each division having a Panzer regiment. Before the end of 1942, these Panzer-equipped units were officially redesignated as *SS-Panzergrenadier-Divisionen* or armoured infantry divisions.

By 1943, the *SS* divisions in action on the Eastern front had been numbered and some had been upgraded to full Panzer status. Those who had taken part in Operation *Barbarossa* became the 1st *SS-Panzer* Division *Leibstandarte Adolf Hitler*, 2nd *SS-Panzer* Division *Das Reich*, 3rd *SS-Panzer* Division *Totenkopf*, the 4th *SS-Panzergrenadier* Division *Polizei*, the 5th *SS-Panzer* Division *Wiking* and the 6th *SS-Gebirgs* Division *Nord*. By the end of the war, there were a total of 38 divisions of the *Waffen-SS*, some having a full strength of 19,000 men in each division, others being considerably smaller.

Many of these new divisions were predominantly manned by foreign soldiers. Only about 12 of the divisions were a true elite; most were formed late in the war and were divisions in name only, often being very poorly equipped.

By 1943, the *Waffen-SS* represented around five percent of the fighting strength of the *Wehrmacht*, though more than a quarter of all Panzer divisions were *Waffen-SS*. The 'classic' *SS* divisions played a significant part in the war on the Eastern Front. Replacements were quickly imbued with the aggressive fighting spirit, and *SS* divisions continued to make great sacrifices until the end of the

war, often holding the line to allow other units to escape destruction.

With the increasing ferocity of combat in Russia leading to greater losses, wartime demand for manpower became insatiable. Recruitment into the *Waffen-SS* was gradually diluted with the acceptance into the ranks of Nordic volunteers and *Volksdeutscher* – people of Germanic descent from countries in Eastern Europe. These were joined by other Europeans and even by Slavic volunteers, who would have been looked on as *Untermenschen* only two years before. By the end of the war, the once 'pure' Nordic stock of Himmler's latter-day Teutonic Knights now included Moslems, Indians

---

# Adolf Hitler said to Leon Degrelle, leader of the Belgians in the *Waffen-SS*: 'If I had a son, I would wish him to be like you.'

---

and Asiatics, intended to make up for the severe battlefield losses and to further expand the *SS*.

The 7th *SS Freiwilligen-Gebirgs* Division *Prinz Eugen* consisted of mainly Croatians and 'a number of Serbs, Romanians and Hungarians. As with many of the later *SS* formations, it was used extensively on anti-partisan duties, and it gained a brutal reputation in Yugoslavia. *Florian Geyer*, the 8th Division, was a cavalry unit. The 9th *SS-Panzer* Division *Hohenstaufen*, 10th *SS-Panzer* Division *Frundsberg*, the 12th *SS-Panzer* Division *Hitlerjugend* and the 17th *SS-Panzergrenadier* Division *Götz von Berlichingen* were the last of the classic SS fighting units.

More typical of later units were the 11th *SS-Freiwilligen Panzergrenadier* Division *Nordland* (manned by European volunteers) and the 13th *Waffen-Gebirgs* Division *der SS Handschar (kroatische Nr 1)*, created largely from Bosnian Muslims in February 1943.

As a further attempt to alleviate the manpower shortage, Himmler increased the upper age limit

LEFT: A *Das Reich* supply column moves forward in the spring of 1942. The winter battle around Moscow had been an appalling ordeal for both *Wehrmacht* and *Waffen-SS* troops. Heavy losses from combat and the cold meant that their attack against the Soviet capital ground to a halt. The *SS* had been trained to be a purely offensive combat formation, but fighting in Russia soon compelled the troops to learn the art of tactical defensive warfare.

of volunteers. This produced a further 40,000 volunteers, most of whom were entering the newly created *Waffen-SS* divisions like the 16th *SS-Panzergrenadier* Division *Reichsführer-SS* and the 18th *SS-Freiwilligen-Panzergrenadier* Division *Horst Wessel*.

In March 1944, a second Latvian volunteer division was formed together with a similar Estonian formation to fight on the Eastern front. In April 1944, Himmler established a new Muslim division named after the great Albanian hero Iskander Beg. The 21st *Waffen-Gebirgs* Division *der SS Skanderbeg* was ready for action in August and undertook policing duties.

Another 14 *Waffen-SS* divisions were created in 1944. They included the 22nd *SS-Freiwilligen-Kavallerie* Division *Maria Theresia*, 23rd *Waffen-Gebirgs* Division *der SS Kama (kroatische Nr 2)*, 23rd *SS Freiwilligen Panzergrenadier* Division *Nederland*, 24th *SS-Gebirgs* Division *Karstjäger*, 25th *Waffen-Grenadier* Division *der SS Hunyadi*, 26th *Waffen-Grenadier* Division *SS Hungaria*, 27th *SS Freiwilligen-Panzergrenadier* Division *Langemarck*, 28th *SS-Freiwilligen-Panzergrenadier* Division *Wallonien*, 29th *Waffen-Grenadier* Division *der SS (russische Nr 1)*, 29th *Waffen-Grenadier* Division *der SS (ital-*

*ienische Nr 1)*, 30th *Waffen-Grenadier* Division *der SS (weissruthenische Nr 1)*, 31st *SS Freiwilligen Grenadier* Division, 33rd *Waffen-Grenadier* Division *der SS Charlemagne* and the 34th *Waffen-Grenadier* Division *der SS Landstorm Nederland*.

In early 1945, the 37th *SS Freiwilligen-Kavallerie* Division *Lützow* were hurriedly assembled and immediately put into the field against the advancing Red Army. However, the division's two regiments were understrength and underarmed, and it was eventually annihilated. A similar fate awaited the final named *SS* division, the 38th *SS-Grenadier* Division *Nibelungen*, which never had a strength of more than 2700 men in its brief existence.

Nothing could now save Hitler's 'Thousand Year Reich'. The volunteer legions that were raised to replace battlefield losses and further expand Himmler's *SS* empire could do nothing to avert catastrophe. By the end of the war, what was left of the *Waffen-SS* divisions went directly from battle into captivity. But unlike the many demoralized *Wehrmacht* troops who shuffled into captivity, the *Waffen-SS* soldiers who entered the POW camps still retained some of their arrogance and defiance even in defeat.

RIGHT: A half track pulls a pair of *Das Reich* Horch field cars along a typically muddy Russian road. It was not only the cold that broke men both spiritually and emotionally, but also the mud. It totally destroyed mobility and its effect had terrible problems for wheeled transport. Even during the encirclement of Kiev, *SS* units were halted by mud and the machines became bogged down. In certain sectors of the front, wheeled transport was either pushed to one side or else, as here, were towed through the worst stretches by tracked and semi-tracked vehicles.

LEFT: Just visible on the rear of the right mudguard of this Horch vehicle is the *Das Reich* divisional insignia. As with most armies, both *Wehrmacht* and *Waffen-SS* vehicles carried such symbols or emblems for easy identification. Most army symbols were issued by OKW (*Oberkommando der Wehrmacht*, or Armed Forces High Command). Most *SS* divisional markings were based on Runic letters, though the *Leibstandarte* used a shield and a key (*dietrich*) to honour the unit's first commander, *Gruppenführer* Josef 'Sepp' Dietrich.

RIGHT: A *Das Reich* dentist extracts a tooth from a Russian peasant while an intrigued little boy looks on. By February 1942, after months of bloody attritional battles, the *Reich* Division was so badly depleted that it was placed in reserve, temporarily being down-graded to a *Kampfgruppe*. After receiving 3000 new troops to replenish its exhausted numbers, the *Der Führer* Regiment was re-equipped as a *Panzergrenadier* unit. In March of 1942, the *SS Kampfgruppe Das Reich* went back into action and took up positions along the River Volga, preparing for a new summer offensive.

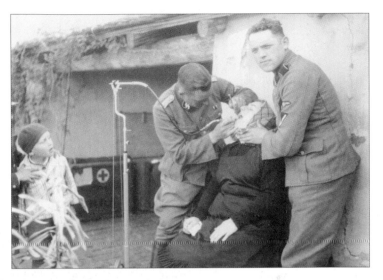

ABOVE: Members of the *SS-Polizei* Division during operations in Russia in the summer of 1942. The *Polizei* Division served with Army Group North, but failed to achieve any real success on the battlefield. However, it did take part in most of the actions around Leningrad. The Germans had arrived within shelling distance of the city in the autumn of 1941, but could not take it and were quickly bogged down by stiffening resistance and the onset of winter. By November 1941, Hitler decided not to waste his troops on an assault of Leningrad, but instead to starve the city out of existence.

LEFT AND OPPOSITE: *Das Reich* troops en route to the front march past their divisional commander, who is taking the salute. The *Das Reich* band plays as the troops march. These men, or what remained of them, were soon to see action along the River Volga, enduring another Soviet offensive in April 1942. Fighting in this region was a brutal contest of attrition and the Germans were undoubtedly hard-pressed to beat back their fanatical foe.

RIGHT: Three *SS* officers confer after a military parade. Note the officer on the right who is wearing the sword and *SS* dagger. Daggers were important symbols to all Nazi organizations, and most wore their own distinctive design. The *SS* dagger was based on that used by the *SA*, from which the *SS* had emerged. All of the men are wearing the high quality officer's greatcoat with *Waffen-SS* issue black belt and aluminium *SS* buckle. Note their M35/40 helmets bearing the right single decal of the *SS* rune. To the left of the men on the parade ground is one of the distinctive *SS* kettle-drums, usually borne in pairs on horseback.

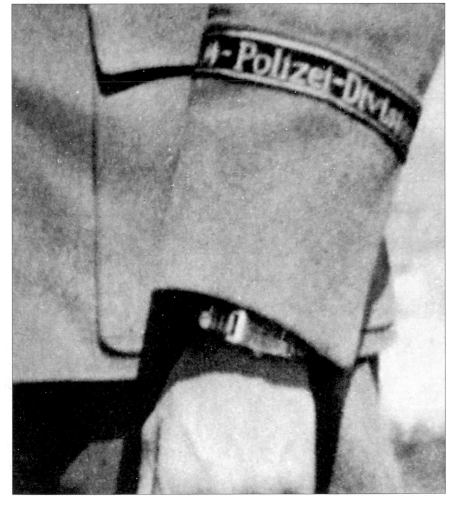

**RIGHT:** The cuff title of the 4th *SS Polizei* Division. Cuff-titles originated in the 19th century. They were awarded as battle honours or to signify membership of an elite unit. During World War II, this was not always the case, however: several *Waffen-SS* formations of dubious ability were awarded titles, as were several units which never even came into existence, while others with fine fighting reputations did not wear them. They were also issued to the personnel of training schools, command staffs or special formations. Several patterns were manufactured and *SS* bands varied slightly in colour, most of them having black cloth with silver gothic lettering and silver edging.

ABOVE: 4th *SS-Polizei* Grenadiers on the front lines around Leningrad in 1942. In August 1942, a new plan for the capture of Leningrad, Operation *Nordlicht*, was drawn up and included an advance across the Neva River to make contact with the Finns east of the city, thereby establishing a closer ring around the former Russian capital. This was to be followed by an all-out assault on the city, supported by more than 800 artillery pieces and heavy aerial bombardment. This grand offensive was scheduled to be unleashed against the city on 4 September 1942. However, the Soviet high command was aware of the steady build-up of hostile forces in the region, and to disrupt the German plan launched a massive offensive of its own. This started in the Siniavino–Mga sector and at Tosno and Uritsk on 27 August.

LEFT: The *Das Reich* band plays as troops march past. Before the war, *SS* units had extensive ceremonial duties, but army gibes that they were simply 'Asphalt Warriors' were quickly forgotten when the *SS* went to war. The organizations's intensive physical and military training, together with powerful psychological indoctrination, finally paid off in Russia. It was a potent force, and the derision of those *Wehrmacht* units that fought shoulder to shoulder with them changed to respect as they kept up fighting long after others had given up the struggle. However, army officers were less impressed by *SS* leadership: they felt that the aggressive *SS* attitude led to unjustified risk-taking and needlessly high casualty bills.

RIGHT AND BELOW: *Das Reich* troops march past their divisional commander as the patriotic tunes of a military band echo along their route. Both the *SS* and the *Wehrmacht* were told that the war in the East would be an easy task, which would be over before winter set in. Most believed that individual Red Army members were discontented with the Soviet system and were badly trained and led by incompetent commanders. However, it soon became apparent that, badly-trained or not, the ordinary Russian peasant was just as ready to die for the *Rodina*, or 'Motherland', as any *SS* man was ready to die for Adolf Hitler.

**ABOVE AND OPPOSITE:** With total military precision, *Das Reich* soldiers wearing their distinctive army issue greatcoats with *SS* runes sewn on the right collar goose-step past their commanding officer. The parade goose step was very demanding physically and was hard to maintain for long. German soldiers used it only at key stages of any parade, such as when they were marching past. Ironically, the Soviets used the same step, having based their ceremonial drill on German manuals. Although the *SS* regarded themselves as a superior force, losses among its units were still heavier than in comparable army formations since many were taking considerable risks, as they had done on the Western Front. However, part of the reason for their high losses was the fact that they were invariably thrown into action where the fighting was thickest. In attack, they lost heavily from snipers and mortars, which were more effective than field artillery, certainly at the beginning of the Soviet campaign. The Soviets had more and better artillery than the Germans, but initially poor co-operation with the infantry nullified this Red Army numerical superiority.

ABOVE: Under the supervision of a motorcyclist, a group of *Waffen-SS* troops, wearing their distinctive camouflage smocks, try to help move a truck out of the mire. The *SS* were not exempt from the trials and tribulations of mud on the Eastern Front. At the height of the *rasputitza*, all wheeled traffic was halted and removed from the road, allowing tracked vehicles to move on their way to the front lines unhindered. However, supplies still needed to be brought forward to the fighting troops, so vehicles had to try to force their way through the mud. Half-tracks were better in the mud than wheeled vehicles or horse-drawn transport, but they were never in good enough supply to solve more than part of the army's logistic needs.

LEFT: The ceremonial face of the *Waffen-SS*. Here a *Das Reich* military band parades with a standard-bearer and infantry colour guard. Looking smart on parade was all very well, but nothing was going to prepare the *SS* for what they endured on the Eastern Front. Frequently an *SS* unit would drive through a seemingly deserted village and swear that they saw neither troops nor inhabitants, but soldiers following up would find themselves facing a fortified position, defended by an infantry regiment and reinforced by all arms.

LEFT: Members of the *SS-Polizei* Division undergo inspection on parade. This photograph was taken in the Leningrad sector early in the winter of 1942. The Soviet offensive unleashed in August had been gruelling, with German soldiers fighting a series of bloody battles to hold their positions around Leningrad. The Germans had managed to blunt the Soviet penetrations through their lines with the sacrifice of thousands of men killed and wounded, but this had in fact absorbed all available manpower sources, which had resulted in the planned assault on Leningrad being abandoned. By this time, the *Polizei* unit had become a fully fledged *SS* division, but it would be some time before its members swapped their mixture of army and police uniforms and police insignia for their *SS* equivalents.

ABOVE: *Waffen-SS* troops rush past a burning Soviet T-34 tank. The easy victories of the summer of 1941 were long in the past: by 1942, it had become obvious that the Red Army would not be defeated so easily. *SS* and *Wehrmacht* soldiers were still confident in their ability to win, but they were now taking seriously the dogged determination of the Soviet soldier, who was remarkable in being able to dig himself in quickly. The Red Army was learning fast: trenches were replaced by deep, narrow foxholes holding two or three riflemen. Machine guns were skilfully sited and trench mortars were available in all calibres, along with many remote-controlled flamethrowers. The Soviet tank forces were still unable to match the Germans tactically, but the excellent quality of their armour would always present the *SS* with problems.

BELOW: Members of the *SS-Gebirgs* Division *Nord* stand on guard inside an igloo during winter operations in 1942. The soldier on the left is armed with a Kar 98k rifle, whilst his comrade is equipped with an MG 34 machine gun. The *Gebirgsjäger* were an elite group of men ready for battle, whatever the conditions. Like their *Wehrmacht* counterparts, these *SS* mountain troops were trained to ski, climb and endure long marches and survive appalling conditions, and were given a role as crack shock troops. Yet in the extreme northern theatre where they fought, they had little opportunity to demonstrate their unique alpine skills. Instead, they were employed as assault infantry or as long-range reconnaissance patrollers.

RIGHT: *Leibstandarte* infantrymen confer beside a Pz.Kpfw.III belonging to the division's tank regiment as they pause in a Russian village. This photograph was taken prior to the III *Panzer* Corps assault on Rostov at the end of November 1941. When the assault finally opened up, snow covered the minefields and the severe arctic temperatures proved a major handicap. But in spite of the severe weather and strong Red Army defences, the division led III Corps in the capture of Rostov. Almost 10,000 prisoners, 159 guns, 56 tanks and two armoured trains were captured. However, the victory was short-lived. The Soviet winter counteroffensive pushed the unit out of the city and back over the river Mius, where the division spent the next two months in intense defensive battles. All but destroyed in the process, *Leibstandarte* was

transferred back to France to rest, recuperate and be rebuilt as a fully fledged *panzergrenadier* division.

ABOVE: An MG 34 team keeps a wary eye out for approaching Soviet troops as winter gradually releases its grip. The war on the Eastern Front was fought in phases: during the summer, the Germans made use of their mobility and armoured power to advance deeper and deeper into Soviet territory. In winter, the Soviets mounted their counteroffensives, using their familiarity with the climate and terrain to hit back at the invader. However, while the *Wehrmacht* was occasionally forced back, the trend was generally a German advance, at least until the end of 1942. Then came the disaster at Stalingrad and the defeat at Kursk.

**ABOVE:** A soldier of the *SS-Gebirgs* Division *Nord* These mountain troops were classed as light infantry, or *Jäger.* As with all such troops, they were highly trained but lightly equipped. Each individual had to carry a considerable amount of kit in his rucksack, but he was also expected to scale mountains or high cliffs as well. The support elements that were integral to traditional infantry divisions, such as armour and artillery, were generally not available to mountain troops. Instead, they were supplied with weapons and other equipment that could be taken apart and man-handled or carried by pack animals. Each soldier had to learn the survival techniques to enable him to survive in the harshest of conditions. He was trained to build a primitive shield of rocks around him, which could protect him against the cold and enemy fire.

ABOVE: Following the inevitable Soviet counterattacks in the Rostov area, German lines are hit hard. Here, an injured *SS* soldier is transported by horse litter through the snow. A *Leibstandarte* soldier jotted down in his diary: 'It is not possible in words to describe the terrible winter on this front. There is no main battle line, no outposts, no reserves. Just small groups of us depending upon each other to hold defended parts. Life here is totally at a standstill. All we live on is a sort of thick soup made of ground buckwheat and millet. We have to strip the fallen, theirs and ours, for warm clothing. I don't think I will ever be warm again and our tame Ivans say that this is a mild wind. God preserve us'.

LEFT: Winter of 1942 – a group of *Gebirgs* troops wearing their distinctive two-piece white camouflage smocks and white-washed steel helmets prepare to move out. The mountain troops were expert in alpine warfare, but it was their ability to operate on skis in severe cold which was of most value. There were few mountains in the far north of the Eastern Front where they were deployed, only seemingly endless forest and featureless Arctic tundra.

LEFT: Ski troops of the *SS-Gebirgs* Division *Nord* advance across deep snow. The authorized strength of a mountain division on paper was 14,000. Added to that were some 5500–6000 animals, including approximately 1500 horses, 4300 pack animals and 550 mountain horses. Divisional equipment also consisted of some 1400 motor vehicles and 600 horse-drawn vehicles. It was armed with 13,000 rifles, 2200 pistols, 500 machine guns, 416 light machine guns, 66 light mortars, 75 anti-tank rifles, 80 heavy machine guns, 44 medium mortars, 16 light infantry guns, four heavy infantry guns, 12 light anti-aircraft guns, 39 anti-tank cannon, 12 light field or mountain howitzers and 24 light mountain guns.

ABOVE: A rare photograph of two soldiers belonging to the *SS-Gebirgsjäger Ausbildungs und Ersatz Abteilung,* or Training and Replacement Battalion. This was formed in March 1942 from the *SS* Replacement Battalion *Nord,* tasked with training recruits and providing replacements for the 6th *SS-Gebirgs* Division *Nord.* Further replacement units were created to provide the same service for the *Prinz Eugen, Handschar* and *Karstjäger* Divisions. There is very little background information on these units, despite the fact that at any given time they would have tens of thousands of troops on strength.

RIGHT: *Totenkopf* troops are compelled to protect themselves against the bitter night ahead with one single quilted blanket. Even by the early winter of 1942, the *SS* were still learning how to deal with some of the problems of winter warfare. The units best prepared for the winter of 1942 were usually the same ones that had had the foresight to organize supplies of winter clothing in the days of the rapid advances during the autumn of 1941. The men of the *Totenkopf* Division were no exception. The division had set up excellent liaison networks through the depots of units under their command, but they still lacked shelter on the front lines. Over the months that the division fought in the Demyansk Pocket, they had to contend with continual Soviet attacks designed to deny them any shelter. Although casualties were high, the majority of those killed did not in fact perish due to the cold.

LEFT: A group of soldiers belonging to the *SS-Gebirgs* Division *Nord* tend to an injured comrade who is about to be transported on sled to a makeshift field hospital. Living and fighting in the arctic circle was very difficult, even for the well-trained men of the *Gebirgsjäger*. By early 1942, a stalemate of sorts had developed along the front lines with the Red Army. Nevertheless, the distances the soldiers had to travel were immense. Wheeled transport was generally useless in the trackless wastes and forests, and often the most effective means of transport was the sled. Shelter, too, posed a huge problem. Finnish instructors taught the Germans many survival lessons, including how to construct native-style shelters. These ranged from simple windbreaks and igloos to Russian-style insulated huts made out of birchwood.

LEFT: An *SS-Gebirgs* soldier uses a saw to construct an igloo. The building of igloos was most effective in the extreme cold of the northern front, but this type of shelter was initially very unpopular with German forces. Even so, the igloo was often the only chance to create adequate shelter when all other forms of cover were unavailable. In fact, the soldiers found to their surprise that thick-packed snow could actually absorb enemy bullets, as well as provide extremely effective insulation against wind. The igloo was not just as a shelter, but could also be used as a temporary defensive position if needed.

RIGHT: A member of the *SS Gebirgs* Division *Nord* takes aim with his MP 38/40 sub-machine gun. All-German mountain troops wore the traditional Tyrolean *Bergemütze* or mountain cap with the edelweiss emblem worn on the left side. The small white flower is native to the Alps, and symbolizes the original home of the *Gebirgsjäger*. From 1941 onwards, the *SS* formed a number of specialist mountain units, including the original Nord mountain division, five further mountain divisions manned by non-German volunteers, and a number of independent *Waffen-SS* mountain brigades and training regiments. Specialist training was carried out at the the High Mountain School of the *Waffen-SS* located in Neustift, in the Tirol.

ABOVE: *Waffen-SS* mountain troops make heavy work of manhandling an artillery piece through the snow. By 1944, there were a total of six mountain divisions in the *Waffen-SS*, though only the 6th *Nord*, 7th *Prinz Eugen* and 13th *Handschar* ever reached divisional size. The specialized nature of their training meant that the cooperation between the mountain troops of the *SS* and *Wehrmacht* was much closer than the hostility so often the norm between more conventional army and SS units. The *SS-Gebirgs* Division *Nord* worked very closely with the 7th *Gebirgsjäger* Division of the *Wehrmacht*, which spent much of the war based in Lappland. *Nord* provided the rearguard for the withdrawal of the 20th *Gebirgsarmee* on its 1500km (930-mile) retreat from Finland to Norway in October and November 1944.

RIGHT: A group of *SS-Gebirgs* troops advance across the snow with horses pulling sleds full of supplies. Uniforms worn by members of the *Waffen-SS* mountain troops were distinguished by their divisional insignia. The 6th *Gebirgs* Division *Nord* wore shoulder patches with the lettering *Nord* written on them. The 'Hagal' Rune – a six-pointed life-and-death rune, like an 'x' overlaid with an 'i' – was painted on the division's vehicles as their tactical symbol.

ABOVE: Late in 1941, *Waffen-SS* troops supported by an armoured column are seen marching through the snow towards Moscow. Within sight of the spires of the Kremlin, the German forces were hit by a massive counterattack commanded by General Georgi Zhukov. Within days, the three principal groups of *Generalfeldmarschal* Fedor von Bock's Army Group Centre, which had fought a desperate defensive action, finally lost contact with each other. Slowly the entire central front began to disintegrate in the snow, isolated and with unusable vehicles, small arms frozen solid, machine guns seized up in temperatures which reached 40°C below zero (-40°F). An *SS* soldier wrote in his diary: 'We were freezing to death in front of Moscow. It was a cold, which numbed and deadened from the feet up until the whole body was a mass of frozen, aching misery. Most of us did not have any clothing to supplement our uniforms except combat overalls. To try and keep us from freezing, we filled the loose folds of the overalls with paper.'

LEFT: Members of the *SS Gebirgsjäger* Replacement Battalion moving supplies by horsedrawn sled. These troops were probably replacement troops for the 6th *SS-Gebirgs* Division *Nord*. The operations being undertaken were in the Scandinavian theatre of war, where the 20th *Gebirgs* Army of *Generaloberst* Dietl served alongside the Finnish army of Field Marshal Mannerheim. From 1943, the division saw extensive action in the provice of Karelia, and fought shoulder to shoulder with members of the 7th *Gebirgs* Division. It would not be until late 1944 that the 6th *SS-Gebirgs* Division, including remnants of the replacement battalions, would be withdrawn from Finland.

LEFT: A posed photograph of a ski trooper belonging to the *SS-Gebirgs* Division *Nord*. As of September 1941, the *SS* Division *Nord* comprised *SS* Infantry Regiment 6 (mot) I–III, *SS* Infantry Regiment 7 (mot) I–III, *SS* Infantry Regiment 9 (mot) I–III, Reconnaissance Unit, Flak Unit, Engineer Battalion, Intelligence Unit, Division Supply Leader, and supply units of the division. The mountain division saw extensive defensive operations in northern Finland near Kiestinki and fought alongside the Finnish Army III Corps. When Finland concluded a separate armistice with the Soviets in 1944, the 6th *SS-Gebirgs* Division then formed the rearguard for the three German corps withdrawn from Finland in Operation *Birke* (Birch). From September to November 1944, the division marched some 1600km (995 miles) to Mo-I-Rana, Norway, where it entrained for the south of the country. After crossing the Skaggerak, the division refitted in Denmark before deploying to take part in Operation *Nordwind* in the Low Vosges mountains of southeastern France.

RIGHT: Troops of the *SS Gebirgsjäger* Replacement Battalion advance across the snow with horse and sled. The mountain soldiers spent long periods out in the cold, either on long marches or reconnaissance patrols on foot or on skis. In spite of their extensive training, nothing could prepare them for the severity of their first Russian winter. Commanders frequently forbade any mountain trooper to light fires by day, so that no evidence of smoke could be seen rising into the icy air. However, by night, fires were absolutely essential. In the weeks of the deepest freeze during winter, it was imperative for even a well-equipped soldier to get under cover by nightfall to avoid the near certainty of freezing to death in the subzero winds howling in from the Arctic.

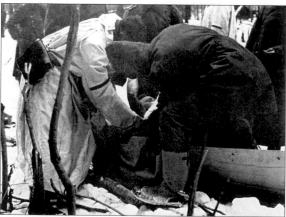

LEFT: *SS* troops unload supplies from a sled sometime in early February 1943, after taking up defensive positions along the Donetz. The imminent catastrophe at Stalingrad meant that on 9 January an *SS Panzer* Corps, comprised of the *Leibstandarte*, *Das Reich* and *Totenkopf* Divisions, was ordered to the Eastern Front. The bulk of the *Leibstandarte* and *Das Reich* was soon concentrated in the city of Kharkov, and then moved up the line. The *Das Reich* Division advanced along the Donetz east of the river, whilst the *Leibstandarte* established a bridgehead at Chegevayev and stretched its grenadiers thinly across the snow for more than 110km (70 miles).

RIGHT: A *Gebirgsjäger* on guard against air attack stands next to his MG 34 machine gun. The weapon is mounted on a *Dreibein* 34 mount, simpler than the more familiar *Lafette* 34 but more suitable for the anti-aircraft role since it could be fitted with extension poles. The weapon could be quickly dismounted if necessary. The double-drum 75-round magazine made feeding ammunition more reliable than loose belts at high angles. The large ring sight was used to calculate deflection angles against moving targets. The gunner is wearing a reversible sheepskin coat with the Tyrolean mountain cap, or *Bergmütze*. Note the Edelweiss badge of the mountain troops sewn to the left side above the ear. Its *Wehrmacht* equivalent was produced only in metal. This type of cap was worn by all ranks of mountain units, ski units and *Jäger* personnel. The cap provided protection from the elements and also shaded the eyes. It was particularly useful against snow glare too. The *Bergmütze* proved to be so popular and successful as a piece of headgear that it was used as the basis for the universal field cap introduced for all ranks in the *Wehrmacht*, *Luftwaffe* and *Waffen-SS* in 1943.

LEFT: An *SS-Gebirgs* officer peers through a pair of periscope binoculars in Finland in early 1942. Given the generic name of *Scherenfernrohr*, or 'scissors' telescopes, these were manufactured primarily by Leitz but were also made by Zeiss. They were used as rangefinders in both world wars. Tripod mounted instruments like this S.F.14.Z.Gi. (*Scherenfernrohr 14 Ziel Gitter* or Stereo telescope, 14 power magnification, with aiming grid) were used by artillery battery commanders and forward observers to make approximate judgement of distances. They were also used in trenches, to allow observations to be made safely from behind cover. This officer more than likely belongs to an artillery unit of the 6th *SS-Gebirgsjäger* 'Nord'. He is wearing a reversible sheepskin coat and the *Bergmütze*. The officer's mountain cap was made from fine quality wool in the early 'blue-grey' shade of field-grey. Although it cannot be seen in this photograph, the cap had a turn-up flap around the body and could easily be lowered to protect the neck and face from extreme weather conditions in a similar way to the contemporary Soviet fur-lined cap, which was also sometimes worn by the *Waffen-SS*.

LEFT: It is late in 1941, and after futile and bloody fighting, infantry and armoured vehicles of the *Leibstandarte* Division withdraw from Rostov, despite Hitler's initial order to fight to the last man. Behind the two *Panzergrenadiers* in the foreground is a StuG.III assault gun. Whilst in the combat zone, the understrength *SS* companies were battling to hold back successive waves of Siberian riflemen storming across the frozen waters of the Mius river. Out on the frozen plain, the *SS* men were easily spotted by reconnaissance aircraft, and suffered devastating attacks by Soviet bombers and artillery. Its performance in the fierce fighting on the Eastern Front won the *Leibstandarte* considerable respect from the army, but the hardness of its men was also reflected in the increasing number of atrocities they committed against the enemy civilians and soldiers. Vengeance was a major motive: over three days in April 1942 the *Leibstandarte* killed some 4000 Soviet POWs in retaliation for the murder of six of their men who had been captured by the Red Army.

RIGHT: *SS Gebirgsjäger* troops advance across the snow with their trusted horse and sled towing supplies. By 1942, the expansion of the mountain troops had begun in earnest. Although the premier mountain division, the 6th *SS-Gebirgs* Division *Nord*, saw service almost exclusively on the Eastern Front, the majority of the *SS* mountain divisions saw extensive service in the Balkans. There they were primarily engaged in the increasingly bitter and bloody partisan warfare raging across Yugolsavia, mainly against Tito's communists, which was a severe drain on German manpower throughout the war. The quality of the *SS* divisions was variable. The 7th *Prinz Eugen* Division was effective, but had a reputation for atrocity. The Muslim division *Handschar* was good enough when led by their German officer and NCO cadre, but when left to their own devices, members were prone to desert to the partisans. The *Skanderbeg*, *Kama* and *Karstjager* units were divisions in name only, never getting above strengths of 3000 men at most and having undistinguished combat records against the enemy.

LEFT: *Gebirgsjäger* officers confer among themselves next to a captured Soviet artillery piece during the early spring of 1942. The gun has received a light application of whitewash paint. Note that the artillery crew have painted parts of the wheels of the gun. This was obviously undertaken when it was standing in its firing position, and helped to conceal the weapon's large black tyres. This particular artillery piece was not widely used by the mountain troops in extreme arctic conditions, as it was too heavy and bulky and required excessive manpower to move it across the snow. However, some units did attach skis to the guns.

# THE *WAFFEN-SS* AT KHARKOV AND KURSK

**The German defeat at Stalingrad early in 1943 caused a major crisis for the *Wehrmacht* in southern Russia. Although there were still *SS* victories to come, the tide was now turning.**

The catastrophic German defeat at Stalingrad in February 1943 changed the face of the war. Panic and confusion swept the disintegrating German lines, and commanders feared the wholesale collapse of the Southern Front. However, despite the reverses suffered as a result of the loss of Stalingrad, Hitler was still confident that he was witnessing the death throes of the Red Army. While most of his commanders were disturbed at the Soviet resurgence, the *Führer* was planning another bold offensive, which he believed would bring final victory. But to do that, he needed to steady the German army, and he looked on the divisions of the *Waffen-SS* to blunt the Soviet offensive. As far as he was concerned, the *SS* had stood firm in the face of adversity – unlike the army. During the winter of 1941–42,

---

LEFT: An *SS* man poses in a trench on the Eastern Front. With him are some Soviet civilians who have been recruited – whether willingly or unwillingly – to help dig German field fortifications.

the *Waffen-SS* had retained its fighting spirit even in defeat. By February 1943, Hitler was determined to use these elite divisions to block the Red Army's drive past Kharkov.

During the first week of February, Soviet forces made a series of deep penetrating strikes towards Kharkov. The attacks were so fierce that on 9 February, during a snow blizzard, the *Das Reich* Division was driven from its positions to a new defensive line on the Donetz. Around the city, German troops clung to a number of scattered strong holds, trying with varying degrees of success to repel the Soviet onslaught. Hitler, as ever determined not to allow Kharkov to fall into enemy hands, ordered that the city be held at all costs. The task of carrying out this *Führer* order was left to *SS-Obergruppenführer* Paul 'Papa' Hausser's newly created I *SS Panzer* Corps.

By 14 February, Soviet troops broke through on to the rear of I *SS Panzer* Corps. A counterattack by elements of *Das Reich* was unleashed immediately, and this temporarily stemmed the Soviet advance. However, by this time it was apparent to Hausser just how futile and costly the fighting had become inside the doomed city. On 15 February, he sought permission to pull his exhausted men out of Kharkov. Later that day, a disgruntled reply came back requesting that the *SS* were to stay put. Hausser was furious with what he regarded as a suicidal order, and chose to ignore the *Führer's* command, instructing the I *SS Panzer* Corps instead to evacuate the now smouldering city.

On 4 March, the I *SS Panzer* Corps and the Fourth *Panzer* Army joined forces under the command of Field Marshal von Manstein. Manstein skilfully withdrew, sucking the Soviets into an extended position before launching a devastating counterattack. Led by the *SS Panzer* divisions, the Germans drove the Soviets back. The *Das Reich* Division made an all out attack and penetrated the outskirts of Kharkov against fierce resistance. To the north, the *Leibstandarte's* *SS Panzergrenadier* Regiments I and II smashed their way into the city.

Fierce urban combat saw some enemy forces escaping the slaughter, only to be annihilated on the Kharkov–Belgorod road by *SS-Totenkopf*.

The victory at Kharkov was now complete. As Hitler predicted, the *Waffen-SS* had shown its skill and determination, spearheading the counterattack and fighting ruthlessly for their *Führer*. However, the capture of Kharkov had come with a heavy price in blood: some 12,000 soldiers had been killed.

With Kharkov retaken, Hitler confidently planned a new offensive against the Kursk salient. Here, Hitler was confronted with a very tempting strategic opportunity that would, he predicted, yield him victory. The Soviets occupied a huge salient, some 190km (120 miles) wide and 120km (75 miles) deep. Hitler told his generals that his forces could attack from the north and south, in a

---

## The Battle of Kursk was the largest tank, air, infantry and artillery battle in history – and it was a turning point in the war.

---

huge pincer movement that would encircle the cream of the Red Army. In Hitler's view, the offensive, code named *Zitadelle*, would smash Red Army power and leave the road to Moscow open. It would be the greatest armoured battle ever fought, utilizing the bulk of the mighty *Panzerwaffe*. As ever, the fight would be led by the toughest of the *Waffen-SS* divisions.

For the offensive, German forces were distributed between the Northern and Southern groups, and consisted of a total of 22 divisions, six of which were *Panzer* and five *Panzergrenadier*. The main attack against the strong Soviet defences at Kursk fell to the 9th Army in the north. But it was to the south of the salient that the *Waffen-SS* was deployed for action. Here, the II *SS Panzer* Corps, commanded by *SS-Obergruppenführer* Hausser, formed part of the 4th *Panzer* Army. The corps comprised the *Leibstandarte*, *Das Reich* and *Totenkopf* Divisions.

On 5 July 1943, as the II *SS Panzer* Corps stood ready to go into action, the pre-dawn light at

LEFT: German field cars get a helping hand from a half-track. A *Das Reich* soldier described what Russian mud was like. 'Following unceasing rainfall, the ground became boggy. According to our maps, we should have good roads, but once the tanks had laboured forward they churned the mud into a morass; any movement of wheeled vehicles was impossible.'

Kursk was shattered by a massive German bombardment. The barrage was so massive that in one hour the German artillery had fired more shells than they had used in both Poland and the Western campaign put together. But despite this violent bombardment, Soviet artillery responded with equal force, and the intense Soviet fire confirmed what all Germans feared: that the attack was not a surprise.

Within hours of the artillery bombardment, the *Waffen-SS* were engaged in the opening stages of the greatest armoured clash in history. The *Totenkopf* Division wasted no time and smashed onto a series of strong Soviet defence lines. The *Leibstandarte* also enjoyed initial success and after hard combat penetrated the first line of defence. The *Das Reich* Division had a promising start as well, and infiltrated enemy lines in front of them. The *SS* divisions were able to wrench open the first line of defences. However, although the *Waffen-SS* made considerable progress, its troops were soon bogged down in a further series of strong Soviet defensive lines. The Soviets had been forwarned of the attack by intelligence sources, and had spent months creating the most heavily defended terrain in history.

In spite of the huge losses the *SS* inflicted on the Red Army, the Soviets reinforced their defences, skilfully deploying mobile armour and antitank reserves to compensate for the high casualty rate. Within days, the Soviets had ground down the mighty *Panzerwaffe*, throwing the German offensive timetable off schedule. By the end of the third day, the II *SS Panzer* Corps had lost 160 of its initial total of 200 tanks, leaving the Corps virtually defenceless. But once again the *SS* demonstrated that they were masters on making do in the face of adversity, and on 8 July repelled a series of armoured assaults at Teterevino, destroying almost 300 Soviet armoured vehicles in just one day.

Despite the fear of being encircled by strong Red Army forces, the *SS* pushed forward along with the 4th *Panzer* Army, attacking northeast of Beregovoy. En route to its objective, on 12 July 1943, the II *SS Panzer* Corps became embroiled in a massive tank battle around the hills of Prokhorovka. This was the climax of Operation *Zitadelle*, which saw the loss of several hundred tanks and thousands of troops from both sides. Ultimately, sheer weight of Soviet numbers along an ever-extending front began to tell, and the German mobile units were finally forced to a standstill. The Germans lost the initiative at Kursk – the tide of victory in the East had finally been turned. But the II *SS Panzer* Corps was not there to see the end of the battle as it fizzled out in ignominy: they had been pulled out of the Soviet Union in order to strengthen the Italian Front after the Allied invasion of Sicily.

ABOVE: A *Totenkopf* grenadier makes the most of the natural environment in February 1943 by constructing a makeshift shelter in a forest. The *Wehrmacht* had endured a terrible winter on the Eastern Front in 1942–43. General Paulus's Sixth Army had been encircled and destroyed at Stalingrad. This Soviet triumph was the signal for the Soviets to unleash a massive offensive in January 1943. The *Wehrmacht* in the south, already worn down by battle and badly depleted by the winter, were pushed back some 480km (300 miles) almost to the Dnieper. As they fell back, they lost the city of Kharkov. It was this city that Hitler wanted at all costs recaptured, and he was determined to use his elite *Waffen-SS* to achieve it.

RIGHT: A soldier belonging to the *Das Reich* Division poses with a group of Russian peasants during the German drive on Moscow, late in 1941. Note the uniform this soldier is wearing. He is far from kitted out with proper winter clothing for protection against the icy blasts to come. His main protection against the cold are the standard issue *Wehrmacht* greatcoat and woollen mittens. As the first winter of the war in the East set in, these garments, designed for less extreme climates, were the only form of winter clothing available to the troops to help keep out of the arctic temperatures. The *SS* at least had their white camouflage smocks. Most German soldiers lined their clothing with paper to provide insulation from the harsh blasts of Russian winter winds.

ABOVE: In contrast to the previous photo, these *Totenkopf* soldiers, seen in 1943, are properly equipped for the winter. These troops formed part of *SS-Obergruppenführer* Paul Hausser's I *SS Panzer* Corps. This photograph was taken during the division's advance on Kharkov, between Kiev and Poltava. Hitler was determined to retake the city of Kharkov at all costs and had planned for the powerful I *SS Panzer* Corps, boasting some formidable armoured forces, to encircle the city and destroy the Soviet armies pushing towards the Dnieper. However, the *Totenkopf* Division became bogged down in mud 40km (25 miles) from their objective, and Hitler was compelled reluctantly to postpone his attack.

ABOVE: Two *SS* troops brave the cold, wearing furs beneath their white winter camouflage smocks. The soldier is using an ammunition box to rest his Kar 98K bolt-action rifle on. This photograph was taken in mid-February 1943, prior to the *Totenkopf* Division joining the rest of the I *SS Panzer* Corps for its attack against Kharkov. Within days, the *Totenkopf* Division would become bogged down in mud. When the division was finally hauled from the mire and reached the rest of the corps, it did not have time to recoup, as the attack was launched almost at once. The armoured regiments of the *Totenkopf*, together with those of *Das Reich*, led the I *SS Panzer* Corps as it smashed into the rear of the Soviet Sixth Army.

RIGHT: A *Totenkopf* MG 34 machine gun team are seen wearing single-piece snow overalls. These items of winter clothing were probably the most popular forms of snow camouflage produced by the Germans. The overall was a single white cotton garment that had an attached hood and long sleeves. Being loose-fitting, it could be easily worn over the uniform and equipment. Whilst the garment afforded complete snow camouflage and excellent freedom of movement to the wearer, it did have one major drawback in that the cotton material quickly got filthy. This photograph shows clearly how much oil and grime the garment could pick up, which possibly reduced the effectiveness of camouflage in the snow.

ABOVE: Two *Totenkopf* soldiers armed with MP 38/40 sub-machine guns. Attached to their belt are M1935 dispatch cases. The soldier on the right also wears one of his magazine pouches on the belt. His comrade has a stick grenade tucked into his belt. By the time this photo was taken, in January 1943, the catastrophe at Stalingrad was reaching its climax. It was now up to

three *SS* divisions, the *Totenkopf*, *Das Reich*, and the *Leibstandarte*, to breathe some spirit back into the *Wehrmacht*. The *SS Panzer* Corps would join the Fourth *Panzer* Army, catching the Soviet armour in a noose. In its wake, Kharkov would fall. It was believed that a six-week respite would follow, allowing the cohesion of the *Wehrmacht* to once more be restored.

RIGHT: *Waffen-SS* mechanized troops take a break from battle. The devastation of the terrain and almost total destruction of surrounding buildings suggests there has been some very heavy combat in the area, or has been laid to waste by *Luftwaffe* aerial bombardment. Note that the railway bridge in the distance still stands intact, indicating that the Germans are advancing – the rail line has been probably spared to allow for it to be used to transport supplies to the front. However, when the Germans began their retreat on the southern front in early 1943, *Wehrmacht* formations devastated the whole countryside. They tore up railway lines, mined roads, blew up bridges and razed towns to make the task of the advancing Red Army even harder.

LEFT: *Waffen-SS* troops interrogate captured Russian prisoners during a pause in bitter fighting near Kharkov. The soldier wearing the white camouflage smock and regulation army-issue camouflage helmet cover is armed with an MG 34 machine gun. Although these Russian troops have evaded death in the battle, the chances that they will survive in captivity at the hands of the *SS* are remote. Tens of thousands of captured Red Army soldiers were executed on the spot rather than taken prisoner, and millions were marched into captivity in the West. If they were lucky enough to survive the march – and tens of thousands of them perished – they had about a fifty–fifty chance of survival in the Reich's harsh labour or concentration camps.

RIGHT: It is late in February 1943 and a *Totenkopf* grenadier poses for the camera during in a lull in the fighting against Red Army forces near Kharkov. It was during this period of the battle against the Soviet 6th Army that the *Totenkopf* were ordered across the endless frozen expanse of the Russian steppe to finish off what enemy resistance was left. By 1 March, it was all but over. Although many Red Army soldiers had managed to claw their way to safety on foot due to the German lack of supporting infantry, the I *SS Panzer* Corps together with the Fourth *Panzer* Army had destroyed the bulk of two Soviet armies. In total they had captured or destroyed some 615 tanks, 400 artillery pieces and 600 anti-tank guns.

ABOVE: *Totenkopf* grenadiers with one of the 615 Soviet tanks captured or destroyed during the battle to retake Kharkov. The *Totenkopf* and *Das Reich* divisions crushed the remaining Red Army armoured formations blocking the path to the city in early March. Once this final obstacle had been cleared, the SS divisions linked up with the Fourth *Panzer* Army for a fierce offensive to take the city. In order to avoid being drawn into a vicious urban battle of attrition,

General Hermann Hoth and Field-Marshal Erich von Manstein decided to take Kharkov by surrounding it. However, as the German armoured units began encircling the city, the commander of the I *SS Panzer* Corps, *SS-Obergruppenführer* Paul Hausser, ignored a direct order to stay out of the city and unleashed his *Waffen-SS* troops, led by the *Leibstandarte*, in an assault into Kharkov. It took three days of bloody street battles to capture the city.

RIGHT: A *Waffen-SS* soldier moves towards a destroyed enemy armoured vehicle dug in at the forward edge of one of the first defensive belts. Although there are no real accurate figures, these Soviet defensive belts were at least 25–30 km (15–19 miles) deep. Each belt consisted of many anti-tank strong points and an extensive network of obstacles. Manning the first defensive belt were some 37 rifle divisions, covering more than 350 battalion defensive sectors. Each sector was spread out up to 6km ($3^3/4$ miles) wide and up to 4km ($2^1/2$ miles) deep, and was defended by a number of these battalions. Divisional sectors averaged a width of 14 km ($8^1/2$ miles) with a depth of 6km ($3^3/4$ miles), with further reserves and artillery units in the rear.

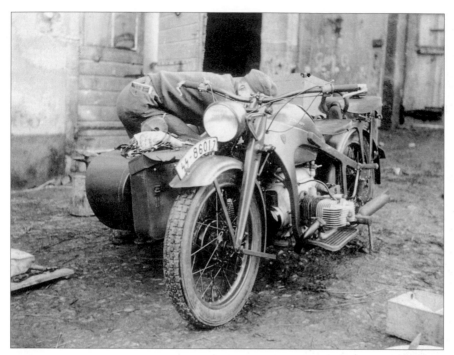

LEFT: A *Waffen-SS* engineer services a motorcycle combination. These vehicles had to travel many hundreds of kilometres across some of the most diverse terrain, and it was very important to keep the motorcycle in good condition. The motorcycle and sidecar aided mobility in areas with good road networks, but they were much less effective on soft ground or on bad roads. The powerful engines that they used were subject to great mechanical strain, and breakdowns were relatively common.

ABOVE: A *Leibstandarte* reconnaissance unit takes a rest in the outskirts of Kharkov late in March 1943, following the successful capture of the city. A medical staff car has halted on the muddy road. With the front in a state of relative calm, the *Leibstandarte* was ordered to undertake security duties in and around Kharkov.

The recapture of Kharkov was the crowning achievement in Germany's successful effort to blunt the Soviet winter offensive – but the *Wehrmacht* had lost much of the ground that it had conquered in 1942. Few Germans could have foreseen that this was to be the last major victory on the Eastern Front.

LEFT: *Totenkopf* grenadiers are seen during a pause in the fighting around Kharkov in March 1943. Three of the men are wearing fur-covered caps that were introduced to both *Wehrmacht* and *Waffen-SS* troops serving on the Eastern Front during the winter of 1942-43. The outside of the hat with its hard liner was covered in field-grey cloth, and it had fur-covered neck and side flaps that could be worn either tied up across the crown of the cap or worn down under the wearer's neck and chin. On the front of the cap, there is a small area of fur across the wearer's forehead. This sometimes displayed a metal or cloth form of the 'death's head' insignia.

RIGHT: *Waffen-SS Panzergrenadiers* move through the outskirts of Kharkov as the spring thaw brings a halt to offensive operations in 1943. The SdKfz 251 half-tracks they are riding were among the first armoured personnel carriers issued in numbers to any mechanized forces in the world. Introduced in 1940, the SdKfz.251 *mittlerer Schutzen-panzerwagen*, or medium armoured infantry vehicle, carried 12 men and their weapons. Built by Hanomag, the 251 was used for a multitude of purposes. Variants included command vehicles, communications vehicles, artillery carriers, multiple rocket launchers, anti-aircraft platforms, and anti-tank weapons carriers.

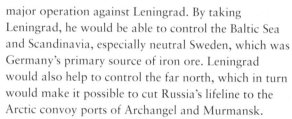

ABOVE: Troops of the 4th *SS-Polizei* Division during operations on the Leningrad Front. Hitler believed that a victory in the Kursk salient would straighten the German front and could be expected to keep the Red Army off balance temporarily. Drawing up plans for the offensive at Kursk, Hitler instructed Army Group North to be ready to follow up the success there with a major operation against Leningrad. By taking Leningrad, he would be able to control the Baltic Sea and Scandinavia, especially neutral Sweden, which was Germany's primary source of iron ore. Leningrad would also help to control the far north, which in turn would make it possible to cut Russia's lifeline to the Arctic convoy ports of Archangel and Murmansk.

LEFT: 5th July 1943, and *Waffen-SS* troops can be seen during the opening phases of the battle of the Kursk, code-named '*Zitadelle*'. Prior to the offensive, German forces had reached their peak strength. The three original SS divisions – *Leibstandarte*, *Das Reich* and *Totenkopf* – were rested, and had been upgraded as fully fledged *Panzer* divisions. Since the capture of Kharkov, they had received 900 tanks and over 300 self-propelled assault guns. The force assigned to the Kursk operation was formidable. General Walter Model's Ninth Army had three *Panzer* corps and two army corps of supporting infantry. In the south, General Hoth's Fourth *Panzer* Army was the strongest force ever put under one single command in the German Army. Operating alongside Kempf's III *Panzer* Corps, his force of six *Panzer* divisions was flanked by three infantry corps comprising nine of the finest German divisions on the Eastern Front.

ABOVE: Late spring 1943, and advancing *Waffen-SS* troops march past a small Soviet POW camp. Following the end of the winter and the spring mud, the German High Command became increasingly worried that the Soviet Army would soon return to the offensive. It was therefore considered, as a matter of urgency, that the German armies would have to strike

first. The area Hitler chose to unleash this offensive was the Kursk salient. By mid-April, Army Group South was to assemble a strong *Panzer* army for an attack north toward Kursk from the Kharkov area. From the north of the salient, Army Group Centre was to create a similar offensive force in the Second *Panzer* Army zone to strike south.

RIGHT: Grenadiers of the *Das Reich* division ride an Sd.Kfz 251 half-track as it passes through a burning village during the initial stages of 'Zitadelle'. On the first day of the attack, it was the task of *Das Reich* to infiltrate enemy lines and soften up the Red Army defences in front of *SS Panzer* Corps. The German forces tried to use their old *Blitzkrieg* formula of using dive-bombers and short, intense artillery bombardment, massed tanks, assault guns and infantry in close contact. Although *Wehrmacht* and *Waffen-SS* started the attack with inferior numbers of armour to their opponents, their Panther and Tiger tanks gave them a definite qualitative superiority. However, even these powerful *Panzers* were unable to deal with the massive Soviet layered defences – line after line of field fortifications sown with millions of mines and manned by 1,337,000 Red Army troops, supported by 3300 tanks, 20,000 guns and 2500 aircraft.

BELOW: An Sd.Kfz 251 half-track moves across the Kursk salient, carrying a section of *Waffen-SS Panzergrenadiers*. At Kursk, the German attack in the north utilized some 335,000 soldiers, 590 tanks – most of which were Pz.Kpfw.III and IVs – and 424 assault guns. In the south, the Germans fielded a much stronger force, concentrating 349,907 of the finest troops in the *Wehrmacht* and the *Waffen-SS*. In spite of Hitler's confidence, many of his commanders were worried at the delay in launching the great offensive. But it was not until the battle started that they realized just how strong their opponent's defences were, and just how many men and weapons the Soviets had been able to concentrate in the area. Clearly, the Soviet high command had known exactly when and where the German attack was to be launched.

BELOW: A group of Sd.Kfz.251 half-tracks have transported *Waffen-SS Panzergrenadiers* to the edge of the battlefield at Kursk. For offensive missions across the battlefield, it was left to the *Panzergrenadiers* to spearhead the attack, clearing ground of enemy infantry and anti-tank guns to allow the armour to advance. The grenadiers scouted ahead of armoured columns, dismounting and deploying against enemy counterattacks while trying to punch their way through enemy defences. Unfortunately for the Germans, at Kursk the Red Army had constructed more than six major defensive belts, each of which were subdivided into two or even three layers of strong, almost impregnable positions. Early German progress was quickly blunted, and as they became entangled in the defences the losses among *Waffen-SS* troops were horrendous.

ABOVE: A StuG.III Ausf. G assault gun armed with a 7.5cm (2.95in) weapon passes a group of well dug-in *SS Panzergrenadiers* during the early phases of Kursk. The assault gun has lost some of its *Schürzen*, or 'side skirts' of armour. The vehicle is finished in dark sand and has a textbook camouflage scheme of green and brown patches applied over the whole of its armour, including the barrel and hull *Schürzen*. With the help of

dive-bombers and anti-tank cannons, the *SS* divisions at Kursk were able to penetrate more deeply than any other formations, in the process repelling a series of armoured attacks. From their starting positions, the *SS* divisions covered a sector more than 20km (12 miles) wide. *Totenkopf* occupied the left flank of the thrust, while *Leibstandarte* moved along in the centre and *Das Reich* held the right.

RIGHT: Two *Das Reich* officers watch as troops unload vehicles destined for the front lines. Moving vehicles by rail was the quickest method of transporting equipment from one part of the front to another. By 1943, however, the organized Soviet Partisan Command had mobilized more than 130,000 guerrilla fighters, whose attacks over more than 2,072,000 square kilometres (800,000 square miles) of territory forced the Germans to divert troops from the front to guard their lines of communications. In fact, during the battle of Kursk, the partisans did everything in their power to interfere with German plans, and the guerrilla campaign in the summer of 1944 contributed in no small measure to the Soviet destruction of Army Group Centre – Germany's largest single military defeat.

ABOVE: *Waffen-SS Panzergrenadiers* move forward past destroyed Soviet T-34 tanks. Although the *Totenkopf*, *Leibstandarte* and *Das Reich* Divisions were able to consolidate their powerful armoured units and knock out large quantities of Red Army vehicles at Kursk, the Soviets still had a considerable numerical advantage. Including reserves, the Red Army fielded nearly 2,000,000 men and over 5000 tanks, an extremely potent array of military hardware. The Soviets were completely prepared for the German offensive at Kursk, thanks to intelligence provided by an extremely effective spy network. The intelligence allowed Marshal Georgi Zhukhov to predict the exact *schwerpunkt*, the strategic focus, of the German attack. For three long months, the Red Army had been busy, building the defences which would receive and then counter the German attack. It was this intelligence, combined with several German postponements giving them more time to build defences, that were to signal the ultimate failure of '*Zitadelle*' even before it had begun.

ABOVE: A few days into '*Zitadelle*' and a group of *Waffen-SS* Pz.Kpfw.IIIs are preparing to move into action. Even though the Pz.Kpfw.III was still present in large numbers in the German inventory, *Panzer* crews knew that even the latest upgunned and uparmoured variants were outclassed. But the *Panzerwaffe* needed desperately to field the maximum number of armoured vehicles for the battle. Although the Ausf. J and Ausf. M were used extensively by both the *Wehrmacht* and *SS Panzer* Corps at Kursk, it was the last great armoured encounter in which the Pz.Kpfw.III was employed in large numbers.

LEFT: An *SS Panzer-grenadier* from the *SS Panzer* Corps keeps low to the ground as a Red Army tank – a T-34 – bursts into flames following a direct hit from a German tank acting in support of the infantry. In spite of the number of Soviet tanks knocked out during the 'Zitadelle' offensive, the Red Army continued to defy the German attackers. An *SS Panzergrenadier* wrote: 'The Red Army soldiers refused to give up. Nor did they panic in the face of our Tigers. The Soviets were cunning in every way. They allowed our tanks past their well-camouflaged foxholes and then sprang out to attack the German grenadiers. Constantly our tanks and assault guns had to turn back to relieve the stranded and often exhausted grenadiers.'

RIGHT: A *Das Reich* officer and his driver pass through a Russian town behind the front line. Between Kharkov in March and Kursk in July 1943, *Das Reich* was in need of considerable reorganization and reinforcement following its heavy losses. The division also had a change of leadership in March after its commander, Herbert Ernst Vahl, was wounded in action. He was temporarily replaced by *SS-Oberführer* Kurt Brasack, who ran the division for a little more than two weeks before relinquishing his command to Walter Krüger. There were no less than 13 divisional commanders of *Das Reich* from 1939 to 1945, two of whom held the position twice.

RIGHT: A self-propelled 3.7cm (1.45in) flak gun seen during *Das Reich's* advance on Moscow. The Soviet Air Force was still recovering from the massive losses it had sustained during the initial German attacks of Operation *Barbarossa*. Nevertheless, aircraft like the Il-2 Shturmovik were a constant threat. However, it is clearly evident from the lack of camouflage and the protective covering over the muzzle that when this photo was taken there was no imminent threat from Soviet air power.

LEFT: The Partisan threat meant that Germans could not relax even when they were located hundreds of miles back from the combat zone. *SS* forces were heavily involved in anti-partisan operations. The first took place in the Balkans, after *Das Reich* and *Leibstandarte* had played such a key role in their conquest. However, most of the *SS* units involved in the bloody, atrocity-prone guerrilla war were drawn fron second-line *SS* divisions and from the *SS* security service – the *SD* – rather than from the fighting divisions. These 'classic' formations were of much greater use on the battlefield.

RIGHT: As became increasingly common in Germany's long retreat from Stalingrad, unit mechanics kept their vehicles running by cannibalizing wrecked or broken-down vehicles. Here, a number of motorcycles and sidecar combinations have clearly undergone the process. In fact, by 1943, when supplies were seriously short following months of heavy fighting, special engineering parties took to the field salvaging vehicles that were fit for cannibalization. The Germans used many types of motorcycle during the war. They included those manufactured by BMW, NSU, DKW and Zundapp, as well as captured Nortons, BSAs, Indians and Harley Davidsons. The despatch rider's motorcycle seen here still displays the faded letter 'G' painted in white on the rear mudguard, indicating that at some stage it was attached to a *Das Reich* motorcycle reconnaissance regiment.

ABOVE: The carnage at Kursk. An *SS* soldier surveys the local terrain through his binoculars, surrounded by destroyed Soviet tanks. Despite continuing to suffer huge losses in both men and weaponry, the Soviets were able to counter Germany's tactical superiority with numbers, and with their own rapidly improving skills. The initial phases of the Soviet defensive action at Kursk were often crude, messy and costly, but in an operational sense they achieved their objectives. They sucked the Germans into a battle of attrition in which the Red Army had the edge. Within a matter of days, they had ground down the once-mighty *Panzerwaffe*.

It was here on the blood-soaked plains at Kursk that, for the first time, the Red Army met a German summer offensive head on and held their ground: until that point, the Germans invariably had the upper hand in summer conflict. But huge though the Soviet force was at Kursk, it was only a portion of what that vast country could put into the field. The end of the Kursk offensive was the signal for the first major Soviet summer offensive: from Smolensk to the Black Sea, the Red Army launched a series of massive armoured attacks. Disregarding all losses, the Soviets continued putting on the pressure until November.

ABOVE: An *SS* grenadier digs a foxhole during a lull in the fighting on the Kursk salient. A StuG.III Ausf. G assault gun passes by, rolling towards the front lines. By 13 July 1943, the Red Army had dealt the *Wehrmacht* a severe battering from which the German war effort was never to recover. The Germans lost 30 of its divisions, including 7 *Panzer* divisions. Some 50,000 German troops were reported killed or missing. '*Zitadelle*' had finally ended the myth of German invincibility. Germany lost 1614 tanks and self-propelled guns in the action. The final nail in the coffin for the German Army was when Hitler decided to withdraw the *Totenkopf*, *Leibstandarte* and *Das Reich* Divisions from Kursk, sending them across Europe to strengthen the Italian Front following the Allied invasion of Sicily.

ABOVE: *SS Panzergrenadiers* stand next to a knocked-out Soviet T-34 during '*Zitadelle*'. This was just one of many hundreds of Soviet tanks destroyed in the battle. *Waffen-SS* tank crews had advanced across the Kursk salient in a succession of armoured wedges, known as the *Panzerkeile*, with heavy Tigers forming the tip of the wedge and the lighter Panthers and Pz.Kpfw.IV's fanning out behind. Grenadiers with carbines and grenades moved close behind these tanks, while

RIGHT: A Pz.Kpfw.IV Ausf. H rolls through a Russian village during *Zitadelle*. At Kursk, the Pz.Kpfw.IV provided the bulk of German panzer strength in both the *SS* and *Wehrmacht* divisions. The three *SS* divisions fielded some 422 tanks and assault guns, of which 170 were Panzer IVs. Although its design dated back to before the outbreak of war, the Panzer IV was still a capable machine, thanks to regular upgrades in its protection and its main armament. Panzer IVs made up the bulk of the German forces used in the great clash at Prokhorovka on 12 July 1943. In this fierce tank battle, which raged for more than eight hours, more than 800 Red Army tanks clashed head-on with 650 *Panzers*. It was a turning point: the Germans failed to make the major breakthrough they needed.

heavier units with mortars followed up at the base of the wedge in half-tracks. The *Panzerkeile* enabled the *SS* to drive deeply in a narrow thrust and was supposed to break down the opposing defensive lines along a considerable length of the front. At Kursk, the *SS* opened each battle with the armour in an infantry-support role, in the hope that there would be enough battle-worthy tanks left to exploit the enemy defences once a breach had been made.

# CAMPAIGNS 1943–44

Following the German defeat at Kursk, which saw extensive losses to the *Panzerwaffe*, German forces fought a series of defensive battles against the increasingly powerful Red Army.

By mid-August, with the Germans desperately trying to hold onto their lines, a massive gap was wrenched open by the Soviets west of Kursk, enabling thousands of troops to pour through. In a drastic attempt to stem the Soviet advance, the *Totenkopf*, *Wiking* and *Das Reich* Divisions were immediately thrown into the battle to prevent the loss of Kharkov. Well-aimed *SS* anti-tank guns managed to knock out some 180 Soviet tanks, but even the determined *SS* legions could only delay the Soviet onslaught. *Wehrmacht* and *Waffen-SS* soldiers were forced to abandon the city on 22 August 1943.

Over the next weeks, the *Totenkopf*, *Wiking* and *Das Reich* Divisions fought a series of skilful withdrawals against numerically superior enemy forces. Again and again, they showed their worth in the field of action. In spite of

LEFT: A *Waffen-SS* officer inspects a defensive position on the Eastern Front in the autumn of 1943. The weapon is a captured Soviet Maxim Model 1910 water-cooled machine gun. It was not as easy to move around as the German MG 34 and MG 42 – on its wheeled mount, the gun weighed 74kg (163lb) – but it was an excellent weapon for fixed defensive roles, being able to maintain fire for long periods.

serious losses in men and materiel, *SS* troops continued fighting with all the ruthlessness and élan that made them such an efficient and lethal weapon of war. However, despite their dogged resistance, they were slowly beaten back towards the Dnieper, culminating in a vicious two-day battle for the town of Yelnya. The *SS* was finally driven back with heavy losses.

The fall of Yelnya signalled the gathering momentum of the Red Army, which went on to capture Bryansk, Smolensk and Roslavl in quick succession. By 2 October, German forces had been driven back some 240km (150 miles).

In November 1943, as the situation worsened on the Eastern Front, the *Leibstandarte* was recalled from Italy and rushed to the Ukraine. It was assigned to XLVIII *Panzer* Corps of the 4th *Panzer* Army, deployed south of Kiev. The city had already fallen, on 7 November, and *Leibstandarte* along with *Das Reich* was thrown into a series of vicious counterattacks.

*Leibstandarte* retreated towards the town of Zhitomir, battling for every yard. At Berdichev, it linked up with the 1st Panzer Division and temporarily halted another Soviet attack. Meanwhile the *Totenkopf* had been used as a 'fire brigade', rushing from one sector of the threatened front to another. In November 1943, it was attached to Hube's 1st Panzer Army, in an attempt to hold a defensive position along the Dnieper at Krivoi Rog.

On Christmas Eve 1943, the Red Army renewed their advance westwards and made a series of savage strikes in the Ukraine. The Soviet advance was so overwhelming that they captured Kirovgrad on 8 January 1944. Soviet commanders quickly implemented plans to resume their westward advance, but they had driven so far and so fast they had outrun their supply lines, and were thwarted by strong German defences. Among the 11 mainly *Wehrmacht* divisions holding a large salient were the *Wiking* and the *Wallonie* brigades, the Belgian Walloon volunteer unit that had been transferred from the Army to *Waffen-SS* control.

The Soviets knew that, in order to ensure the success of their offensive, they needed to destroy the German forces in the salient. On 25 January, the Red Army launched a massive attack, and within four days some 60,000 German troops had been encircled near Cherkassy.

Constant pressure was maintained on the encirclement, and although there were frantic appeals by German commanders to be allowed to retreat, Hitler would not listen, insisting that his forces remain in place. However, following days of futile and costly combat inside what became known as the 'Cherkassy Pocket', Hitler finally agreed on a breakout.

During the evening of 16 February 1944, the breakout began. The *Wiking* Division, the only

---

## The Soviet summer offensive of 1944 was the largest in history as front after front, army after army launched a wave of attacks against the crumbling German defences from Leningrad to the Crimea.

---

armoured unit in the pocket, was given the task of covering the flanks, while *SS-Sturmbrigade Wallonie* formed the rearguard. Movement was painfully slow as the troops slogged across the boggy terrain. Soviet artillery quickly took advantage of the situation and laid down a huge barrage of fire on the Germans. The fire was so intense that almost 70 per cent of the *SS-Sturmbrigade Wallonie* was wiped out. The remnants of the *Wallonie* units that had not already been blown to pieces or had been left badly wounded in blood-soaked trenches, fought on with typical *Waffen-SS* self sacrifice. Thanks to these men, almost 32,000 German soldiers managed to escape almost certain devastation and death in the pocket.

A major disaster had been averted. The *Wiking* Division, having been all but wiped out at Cherkassy, was withdrawn from the Eastern Front and sent near Warsaw to rest, recuperate and rebuild its numbers.

Elsewhere on the Eastern Front, the *Waffen-SS* continued in its attempt to stem the Soviet onslaught. Around Leningrad, *SS* volunteer units were deployed to prevent a breakthrough. The main *SS* forces in this sector consisted of the 11th *SS-Freiwillgen* Division *Nordland* and *SS-Freiwillgen* Brigade *Nederland*. Volunteers in these two units included men from Denmark, Holland, France, Finland, Switzerland and Sweden. Other *Waffen-SS* 'foreign legion' units included the 15th and 19th *Waffengrenadier* Divisions from Estonia and the Flemish *Langemarck* Brigade. These troops were dug in to strong defensive positions around the strategically important city of Narva.

The vicious fighting that took place around this city on the Baltic coast became known as the 'Battle of the European *SS*'. It began early in February 1944, with Soviet artillery opening up a massive bombardment in an attempt to soften up the German defences. Red Army units soon forced a crossing near Narva, but the *SS* were able to throw them back across the river. The Soviets were nothing if not persistent, and after a series of attacks they unleashed a seaborne assault with a motley collection of fishing boats and steamers. *Waffen-SS* grenadiers were yet again roused from their dugouts and were initially able to keep the attacking enemy from making progress, though fighting in some places

was so severe that it degenerated into hand-to-hand combat.

Terrible battles continued to rage through March and into April, with the Red Army being constantly blocked by stubborn *Waffen-SS* resistance. However, it soon became clear that the Soviets could not be held for much longer. With Soviet strength increasing almost daily, *SS* commanders decided in June 1944 to pull back their troops to a new defensive line further west, which became known as the 'Tannenberg Line'. But this battle, fierce though it was, soon became a sideshow.

On 22 June 1944, the Soviets launched their summer offensive. Operation 'Bagration' was deliberately timed to begin on the third anniversary of the German invasion of Russia. From Velikie Luki in the north around a huge arc to Kovel below the Pripet Marshes, the artillery of four Red Army fronts – 15 armies – crashed out, while the aircraft of four air armies flew overhead. Their objective was simple: to obliterate Army Group Centre. Zhukhov's armies tore a 320km (200-mile) hole in the front. Whole armies were encircled as the vengeful Red Army drove westwards. The destruction of Army Group Centre was Germany's worst disaster of the war – worse than Stalingrad. In weeks, 28 divisions had been totally destroyed, and more than 350,000 men had been killed or captured.

LEFT: *Waffen-SS* troops, part of Army Group South, in action on the Eastern Front during the summer of 1943. Following the disaster at Kursk, the majority of *Wehrmacht* and *Waffen-SS* units were seriously under-strength, and were being still further depleted by continuous combat. The only force available that was in better shape than the regular *Panzer* divisions was the *SS Panzer* Corps, but this had been withdrawn from the battle of the Kursk to help prop up the Italian Front. However, before it could be sent, Hitler finally recognized the true state of affairs in the East and only the *Leibstandarte* actually left by train for Italy. The *Das Reich* and *Totenkopf* Divisions were returned to the front to fight a series of battles against an offensive that the Red Army had launched along the River Mius in late July 1943.

LEFT: On board a railway flat car, an *SS* Tiger crewman makes sure one of the Pz.Kpfw.VI Tiger I Ausf. E tanks is secure by nailing a piece of wood in front of the tank track. One of the main factors in the success of *SS-Panzer* divisions on the Eastern Front was the speed with which they could be transported from one sector of the front to another. On many occasions, the Red Army boasted that they had annihilated the *Panzer* division, only to find weeks later it had reappeared hundreds of miles away. What in fact had happened was that the division in question was being used as an emergency 'fire brigade' and had been withdrawn from the front line to be transported by rail to another area of Russia.

ABOVE: An *SS* flak crew in action on the Southern Front during the summer of 1943. Throughout the second half of 1943, the *Wehrmacht* was in steady decline. In the three months following the disaster at Kursk, General von Manstein's army group received only 33,000 replacements, in spite of having suffered nearly 140,000 casualties. The equipment situation too continued to deteriorate, especially in the *Panzer* units.

However, despite incurring massive losses, it was the *Waffen-SS* that continued to receive the best tanks and assault guns for its own divisions – a marked contrast to the early days of the war, when the *SS* received its equipment grudgingly from the army. But good equipment was not enough: while their own numbers and firepower remained static or declined, the Red Army was getting larger and more powerful by the day.

ABOVE: A rear view of a late variant of the long-serving Pz.Kpfw.IV, being operated by a *Waffen-SS* unit during operations on the Southern Front. In spite of huge losses inflicted on the *Panzerwaffe* at Kursk and through the rest of 1943 and 1944, the Pz.Kpfw.IV still played a prominent role in the *SS* regiments. All along the front lines, they fought desperate defensive actions to halt the Red Army. Although the Soviet forces enjoyed overwhelming numerical superiority, *SS* Pz.Kpfw.IV crews were not deterred by the seemingly endless losses, and carried on holding the line. In well-trained hands, the Panzer IV could still hold its own. The 5th *SS Panzer* Division *Wiking*, for instance, was primarily armed with the tank, and it distinguished itself by holding the flanks of the Cherkassy Pocket as 30,000 Germans escaped almost certain death.

ABOVE: An injured *Panzer* crewman decorated for his skill and bravery in the face of growing armoured opposition. Until the invasion of Russia, German tank crews had enjoyed tank superiority, but from then on the situation was reversed as crews first started coming across the T-34 tank. The prospect of rapid decisive victories soon faded, and the *Panzerwaffe* cried out for a new tank with a formidable mix of firepower, armour and mobility to deal with the Soviet tank threat. Based on similar design principles to the T-34,

the Pz.Kpfw.V Panther tank was more powerful than the T-34, but it was rushed into action prematurely at Kursk. Once the teething troubles were sorted out, the Panther proved to be an outstanding, if expensive and complex, machine. On the open steppes of the Eastern Front and also in the west, the *SS* found that the Panther repeatedly proved itself against the huge Soviet armies and against the Anglo-Americans in Normandy. But neither it nor the heavier Tiger were ever available in the numbers required.

LEFT: A group of *Waffen-SS* troops wearing their reversible grey/white winter suits stop for a break behind the cover of a knocked out Soviet T-34 tank. The men are also wearing the heavy felt and leather boots, German items that were considered superior to the Soviet felt boots on which they were modelled. These white camouflage suits were efficient garments and were still very popular in the ranks of the *Waffen-SS* in 1944–45. However, the soldiers regularly complained about the integral hood that restricted vision, and it was not normally worn up over the helmet except in the worst conditions.

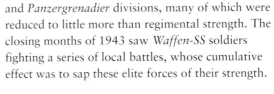

ABOVE: *Waffen-SS* troops survey the destruction of a Red Army position in southern Russia in the winter of 1943. These soldiers formed part of the southern front. To protect 725km (450 miles) of front, the Germans had only 37 infantry divisions and 17 *Panzer* and *Panzergrenadier* divisions, many of which were reduced to little more than regimental strength. The closing months of 1943 saw *Waffen-SS* soldiers fighting a series of local battles, whose cumulative effect was to sap these elite forces of their strength.

LEFT: Moving out from beneath the shelter of a destroyed T-34 tank, an *SS* soldier goes into action. The T-34 was fast, well armed and manoeuvrable. Its wide tracks were excellent for dealing with snow or mud, and its sloped armour made it difficult to knock out. Nevertheless, between 1941 and 1943 large numbers of T-34 tanks were destroyed by the mechanically inferior but tactically superior German *Panzer* forces, and the emergence of the Tiger and Panther promised qualitative superiority as well. Unfortunately for the *Wehrmacht* and the *Waffen-SS*, German industry could not match the massive production of the Soviet tank factories in the Urals, and Soviet tank designers redressed the balance further by fitting the T-34 with a more powerful 85mm (3.34in) gun. The T-34/85 was to remain the principal Soviet tank for the remainder of the war.

LEFT: A soldier of the *Das Reich* Division seen during defensive fighting near Kiev. By early November 1943, *SS-Panzer* Division *Das Reich* had been ground down to a fraction of its former size. Much of the shattered remnants of the division withdrew to France to rest and refit: a nucleus of the division remained active in the East as *Kampfgruppe Lammerding*. This consisted of some 5000 soldiers, including an infantry regiment with the 1st Battalion, *Deutschland* Regiment and 2nd Battalion, *Der Führer* Regiment. It also had an armoured battalion that included two *Panzer* companies, a Reconnaissance Battalion, two SP artillery companies, a pioneer company and various heavy weapons units. This new *Kampfgruppe* continued to fight on the Eastern Front for several months, eventually rejoining the rest of the division in the south of France in April 1944.

BELOW: An *SS* Flak crew wheels a 2cm (0.78in) Flak 30/38 through the mud on the Eastern Front. Capable of engaging targets at ranges of 4800m (5250yd) (ground) and 3700m (4050yd) (air), this light anti-aircraft gun served from the Spanish civil war to the end of World War II. Effective against soft targets, it was less so against armour, and had some difficulty in pen-etrating the heavily protected Soviet Il-2 *Shturmovik* ground attack aircraft. Each front line *SS* division had a flak *abteilung* of between 800 and 1200 men, with a mix of light, medium and heavy AA guns – typically a battery of six 8.8cm (3.45in), 2 batteries of four 3.7cm (1.45in) and several batteries of 2cm guns, later supplemented by *Flakvierling* quadruple flak mounts.

ABOVE: *Waffen-SS* troops prepare to go into action with a 7.5cm (2.95in) *leichte Infantriegeschutz* 18. L/11.8 gun. This weapon was developed by Rheinmetall, and was the first new artillery piece to become standard issue for German infantry units after World War I. This photograph was taken on the southern part of the Eastern Front, probably in early autumn of 1943. By November, both *Wehrmacht* and *Waffen-SS* divisions were faced by massive Red Army pressure towards Kiev. *Das Reich* saw extensive action as the Soviets continued to push the German armies westward out of the Ukraine. The *Totenkopf* were also given the gruelling task of slowing down the Red Army advance, while the *Leibstandarte* had been rushed back from the Italian Front to try to cut Soviet supply routes between Kiev and Zhitomir.

LEFT: A *Totenkopf* radio operater uses his light-weight, sled-mounted radio set. He is probably at a forward observation post, from where he can send details of enemy movements back to divisional headquarters. In spite of its mauling on the Southern Front during the second half of 1943, the *Totenkopf* division continued to be a first-class fighting formation. Indeed, it was continuously called upon to provide a rearguard as the Germans withdrew successively from the Dnieper, Krivoi Rog and Kirovgrad. In March 1944, the division was airlifted to Balta to protect Army Group B's retreat to the Dniester River on the border with Romania.

RIGHT: An *SS* soldier well-protected from the extreme arctic temperatures. He is wearing the standard equipment for a rifleman with the usual belt and cartridge pouches. The cold affected almost everything the Germans used and this made life, especially the first winter on the Eastern Front, very difficult. The arctic temperatures made it necessary for the troops to use any means possible to overcome the immense problems they faced in a subzero environment. New lubricants were made available to replace standard ones, which tended to freeze solid in the actions of rifles and machine guns. Sunflower seed oil was widely used by the *SS*, and became the standard German rifle oil. Other lubricants included finely-ground powders: some *SS* units found that finely textured flours of sulphur were particularly effective and troops were regularly seen sprinkling it on their weapons to ensure a smooth bolt action.

ABOVE: An orders group forms up on the Eastern Front as a divisional commander passes instructions on to his subordinates. When allowed to fight unhampered, the Germans proved to be masters of the fighting retreat, giving up ground to the enemy and then mounting stinging counterattacks. However, Hitler could never see the use of such tactics, usually ordering his units to fight where they stood. Without the option of flexibility, units suffered horrendous casualties in bludgeoning Soviet attacks, and by the time Hitler could be persuaded to allow a withdrawal, it was usually too late for an effective counterattack to be launched. Officers who retreated on their own initiative were usually sacked.

LEFT: A *Totenkopf* signals operator receives orders through his earphones and jots down the messages on his notepad. Although the *Totenkopf* Division lost a great many men in the retreat from Russia, it received more replacements than most divisions in the field on the Southern Front. It was in constant action against repeated Soviet attacks, and actually contained Soviet units in a number of places. One such large defensive campaign was when the *Totenkopf* prevented the Red Army from capturing Krivoi Rog for nearly two months before the city finally fell. Retiring to Romania, the division received 4500 replacements from the 16th *SS* Division, and by May 1944 it was fully up to strength with 21,000 men.

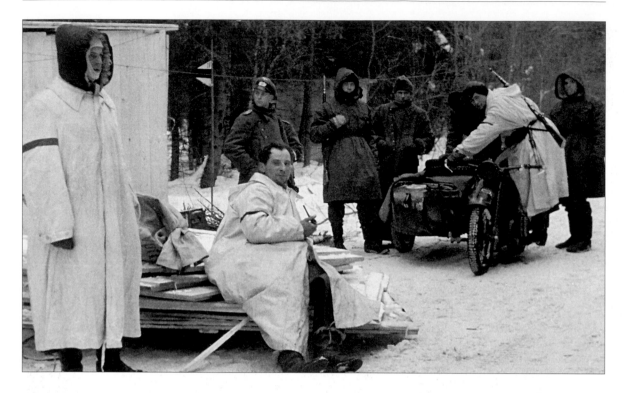

ABOVE: A group of *Waffen-SS* soldiers pose for the camera early in 1944. Although *SS* units continued to fight hard to hold their positions, they were constantly subject to intense bombardments by whole divisions of Soviet artillery. Difficulties of terrain hindered communications between the units, and defences that were too thinly spread allowed the Soviets plenty of weak spots through which to infiltrate. *SS* soldiers regularly found themselves cut off and having to fight for their very existence. Relief efforts were patchy: supply units could not keep pace with the fighting and more and more supply vehicles succumbed to the appalling weather and road conditions before reaching the units they were meant to supply. Cut-off troops had the option of fighting to the death or of breaking out through the surrounding Soviet armies.

LEFT: Dressed in their winter white camouflage smocks, *SS* troops trudge along a frozen road, passing dead Soviet soldiers lying in the snow. The Red Army was basically an infantry force with a primitive supply and administration service, manned by soldiers of immense toughness and physical strength, which enabled them to carry heavier loads for longer distances than most. They were accustomed since birth to far colder temperatures, which they withstood on far smaller rations than many in the West would have believed possible. Faced with such a foe, the German soldier had to adapt very quickly, or die. The snow and then the thaw offered great obstacles to the troops' mobility, but eventually they found ways to overcome some of the problems.

ABOVE: German soldiers sometimes found that road travel in Russia was easier in winter than in summer, so long as the surface was kept free of snow. Both the *Wehrmacht* and *Waffen-SS* employed local gangs of civilians to clear the roads with shovels. These snow battalions, as they were nicknamed, were not committed until the blizzards or snowstorms had covered a road. Once at work, the snow battalions could quickly clear long stretches of highway. The Germans also learned that snow lay less steeply in woods and forests, making travel easier. To increase the number of passable routes for men and equipment in these conditions, the snow battalions were regularly ordered to make alternative routes through forests or along hillcrests and ridges, where the snow did not build up to form huge drifts.

ABOVE: In action against Siberian Ski troops, a *Waffen-SS* mortar crew prepare to fire a shell. Because *SS* troops were often used as special fire brigade units, being moved from one disintegrating front to another, fighting rearguard actions as often as not, inevitably there were times when they became encircled and had to undertake daring breakout operations using just their own resources. Usually the whole encircled body rolled through enemy lines as a kind of mobile pocket, driving westwards to regain their own lines. In these conditions, with no chance of resupply, food was rationed and fire discipline kept tight in order to conserve ammunition. The *SS* principle was to select one point of the encirclement and to channel every force to that place. It usually fell upon the grenadiers to reconnoitre and clear the route ahead.

LEFT: *SS* troops in full winter kit prepare to move out to do battle against Red Army ski troops. In an attempt to defeat the terrible cold, some of the men are wearing the woollen toque, scarf and gloves. Hooked to each soldier's Y-straps is the webbing assault pack consisting of an A-frame to which are attached their mess tin, gasmask canister (rarely carrying a gas mask) with gas cape, personal kit and ration bag, and rolled *Zeltbahn*. Hanging from the belt are the soldier's bread bag, water bottle and entrenching tool, with a Mauser 98K bayonet strapped to its carrier.

RIGHT: A *Waffen-SS* unit on the move. By 1944, the Red Air Force had the advantage over the *Luftwaffe* in the skies, and Soviet fighters and bombers regularly dropped incendiary bombs on any forms of shelter used by the Germans. This could include complete villages and towns, which were devastated without regard for the cost to their inhabitants. A number of *SS* units chose to live out in the open, although living in such extreme temperatures without shelter not only caused acute problems for the men, but also caused terrible problems with equipment. Oil and grease froze in the recoil systems of artillery pieces, even those covered by heavy tarpaulins. Frozen breechblocks had to be heated before they could be opened. Fires had to be lit under vehicles to thaw petrol which had frozen. During the early winter of 1944, some soldiers remarked that with the dwindling supplies, 'everything we had mastered to combat the problem of winter warfare was useless, and our position was more like what we had suffered in those terrible winter months in front of Moscow in 1941'.

ABOVE: *SS* soldiers set up a temporary position for the night deep in a forest during a lull in the Red Army advance in 1944. Although the front might have felt comparatively quiet during a lull, the troops were well aware of the constant dangers of suddenly being attacked by a Soviet night patrol. In order to keep relatively mobile in the snow, the troops are using sleds to pull their supplies. As soon as the winter nights closed in, the temperatures began to plummet even further. It was therefore imperative to have set up some kind of shelter before nightfall. Even their woollen greatcoats, reversible anoraks, sheepskin coats, fur caps and felt boots could not prevent the cold from slowly chilling them and bringing the risk of exposure. Every man knew that a bad wound meant death in the freezing temperatures.

RIGHT: A signals unit in operation early in 1944. By the spring, the Soviet High Command planned to follow up the southern offensive with a series of equally massive attacks down the whole length of the Eastern Front. At the heart of the strategy was Operation 'Bagration', intended to destroy Army Group Centre, which still occupied the most important sector of the Eastern Front. This guarded the route to Warsaw, and was on the high road to Berlin. Time was running out for *Waffen-SS*, *Wehrmacht* and foreign legion troops. A threat on the Western Front was also looming, as the long awaited Anglo-American invasion threatened Germany's nightmare: all-out war on two fronts.

LEFT: Fighting continued with unabated ferocity as the *SS* tried to block the advancing Red Army juggernaut, or at least slow its progress. Few other units could have endured or shown such confidence in the face of such overwhelming odds, but the soldiers of the *Waffen-SS* still continued to fight for their *Führer*. A *Wehrmacht* soldier watched with amazement as *SS* troops saved his entire regiment from catastrophe when it was under fierce attack from the Red Army. He noted in his diary: '…They came forward with daring *élan*, plugging our decimated lines armed with a motley collection of MG 42 machine guns. Here they held a position for three hours against strong Red Army infantry, allowing our exhausted and badly depleted forces to escape from almost certain destruction. We are forever indebted to these men, men that deserved a laurel wreath for their sacrifices.'

RIGHT: An *SS* MG 34 machine gun team open fire against enemy positions in the snow. Both 1943 and early 1944 had seen a series of terrible disasters for German arms, but the *Waffen-SS* had stood resolute. By the end of 1944 even the most fanatical of *SS* troops must have been aware that the end was approaching, with huge armies closing on the Reich from East and West, yet pride led them to make sacrifice after sacrifice, fighting to hold the line to allow other units to escape the impending doom.

ABOVE: A brief respite during a fighting withdrawal. Within weeks, these men would be trying to contain yet another massive Red Army attack. Between March and mid-April, the spring offensive on the southern front was unleashed, sending *Wehrmacht* and *Waffen-SS* forces reeling back some 265km (165 miles). Those units that braved the enemy onslaught and dug in to try and hold the Soviet stampede were simply cut off and annihilated. The Soviet offensive recovered some of the most productive territory in the Soviet Union, and inflicted massive destruction on Army Groups A and South. But an even greater catastrophe was to come in the summer, as the largest offensive in history burst like a tidal wave around Army Group Centre.

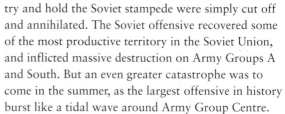

LEFT: A group of *SS* soldiers discuss the situation at the front. Even though the *Waffen-SS* was growing explosively as Himmler took on volunteers and conscripts from all over Europe, only 12 *SS* divisions out of the total of 38 could actually be called elite formations. The rest, mostly created in 1944 and 1945, were generally poorly trained and equipped. Many were divisions in name only. And the enemy had changed, too. The average Red Army conscript was no longer the poorly trained and badly equipped peasant that had entered the front lines in 1941. The huge Red Army of 1944 was formed round a core of experienced veterans, well-equipped with sometimes crude but generally effective small arms, armour and artillery.

RIGHT: *Totenkopf* troops in full winter kit prepare. Note that all the soldiers are wearing rolled ground-sheets that are probably from captured Soviet stocks. Living in the snow was generally very difficult, but all the soldiers were taught that the snow could also serve as an ally, and was not simply an enemy to be feared. Snow was wind-resistant and could act as windbreaks to protect engines of parked vehicles. It was easy to dig trenches, especially communication trenches (although the rock-hard frozen ground beneath was another matter: digging trenches in that called for explosives). The snow also proved to have excellent camouflage properties and the trenches could easily be concealed, as no freshly dug mounds of soil could betray the position.

ABOVE: Sitting on a mound of snow, two soldiers pose for the camera. Note the soldier on the left wearing German versions of the Soviet-style felt boots. Although many *SS* units had fought superbly in battle, there was nothing that they could do to stop the Soviet tide. Even the premier *Waffen-SS* divisions were being ground down in battles of attrition. Their supply lines were stretched to the limit and beyond, and Germany did not have enough men of military age to make good battle losses. The Soviets had more men, more guns and more tanks. The prospects for the *SS* and the rest of Germany looked very grim indeed.

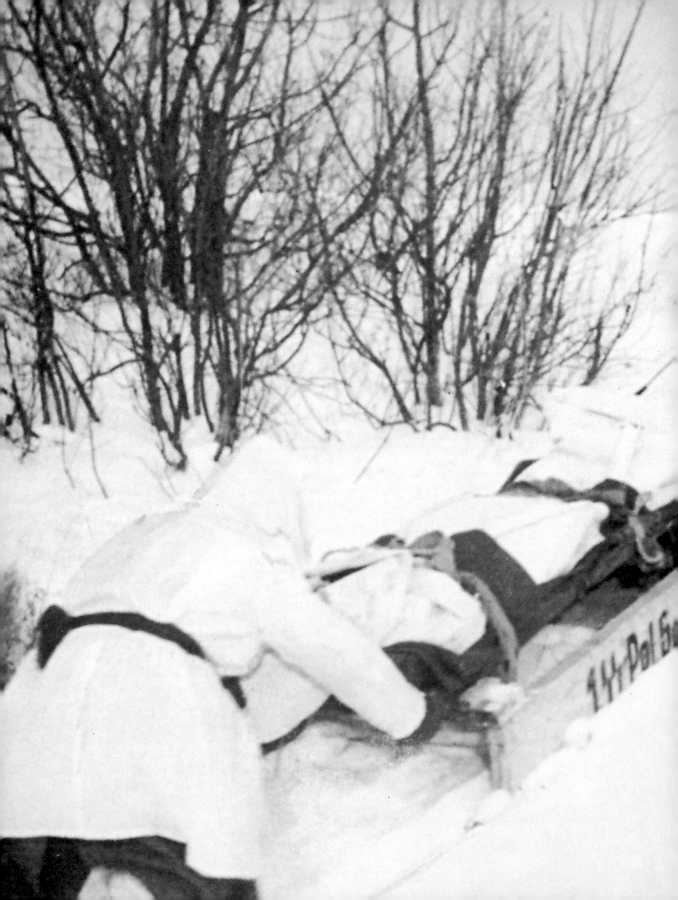

# THE FIGHTING WITHDRAWAL

In June 1944, the *Waffen-SS* found itself in both frontlines of Germany's fight for survival. The Western Allies had landed in Normandy, but the real hammer blow was to come in the East.

For the Red Army's summer offensive, codenamed 'Bagration', the Soviets had amassed a titanic force of some six million soldiers. Germany could muster only two million troops to counter the Eastern Front assaults. Bearing the full brunt of the heaviest Soviet thrust was Army Group Centre, a powerful force fielding some three-quarters of a million men, 10,000 artillery pieces and 1000 tanks. But this was dwarfed by the combined weight of four Soviet Army Fronts – over two million soldiers, 29,000 guns and 4000 tanks.

LEFT: An injured soldier of the 4th *SS-Polizei* Division is evacuated during the unit's withdrawal in Army Group North in the winter of 1944. Here in northern Russia, the Red Army had finally relieved Leningrad, then gone over to the offensive. Slowly the Soviets drove the Germans westwards towards Estonia and Latvia. By the end of January 1945, Soviet forces had reached the German defence line at Narva, where the foreign volunteer units of the *Waffen-SS* were to fight what became known as the 'Battle of the European *SS*'.

On 22 June 1944, the Soviet offensive was unleashed with Bagramyan's First Baltic and Chernyakovsky's Third Belorussian Fronts attacking northwest and southeast of the city of Vitebsk. The assault took the German Third *Panzer* Army completely by surprise. The next day, the Red Army tore through the Third *Panzer* Army and closed in behind Vitebsk. Within five days, no less than five German divisions were encircled. Desperate *Wehrmacht* and *Waffen-SS* troops began to claw their way out of the cauldron. Remnants of the five divisions withdrew westward, retreating under a tumultuous Soviet ground and air bombardment.

The collapse of Army Group Centre continued with the encirclement of Mogilev by Zakharov's 2nd Belorussian Front, and of Bobruisk by Rokossovsky's 1st Belorussian Front. Columns of fleeing German vehicles choked the roads west, under continuous air attack.

In just 12 days, Army Group Centre had lost 25 divisions, and the Russians had torn a massive hole in the front. By 4 July, both Zakharov's and Chernyakovsky's Fronts had driven forwards over 200km (125 miles), leaving only one pocket of German resistance, which surrendered on 11 July. The momentum never flagged; everywhere the Germans were in full retreat.

The destruction of Army Group Centre was a far greater disaster than that which had befallen the Sixth Army at Stalingrad. Of its original strength of 165,000 men, Fourth Army lost 130,000. The 3rd *Panzer* Army lost 10 divisions. The 9th Army had wrenched open a pocket to allow some 10,000–15,000 of its troops to escape westward.

For the next few weeks, both *Wehrmacht* and *Waffen-SS* troops withdrew, turning and striking back viciously when they could. Towns and villages were islands of rubble and twisted steel in a devastated countryside. In the burning ruins of towns and cities, the Germans created 'killing zones', where small bands of well-armed *SS* soldiers defended every yard with machine guns, mortars, grenades, flamethrowers and explosive charges. Approaches were also heavily mined. However, in spite of the terrible cost, the Red Army troops continued to inch their way forwards. To the weary, dirty and dishevelled *SS* soldiers, the thought of surrendering now after shedding three years of blood on the Eastern Front seemed unthinkable.

By mid-July 1944, Army Group Centre had been forced back towards Kaunus, the Neman River and Bialystok. The whole German position in the East was on the point of disintegration, and any task of repairing it was made almost impossible by a crippling shortage of troops.

*Waffen-SS* troops continued desperately trying to fill the dwindling ranks. In the northern sector of the Eastern Front, German, Swedish, Estonian, Latvian, Dutch, Flemish, Danish, and

---

## At the end of July, General Guderian made a succinct note in his diary. 'Army Group Centre', he wrote, 'has ceased to exist.'

---

Norwegian *SS* soldiers continued resisting as they retreated. For miles, refugees clogged the already congested roads. Intermingled with this mass of humanity were soldiers, policemen, airmen, sailors, and *SS* soldiers, all trying to escape the impending slaughter.

Red Army troops now surged deep into Poland and by the end of July they were approaching Warsaw. It was here that the *Totenkopf* Division was given the task of shepherding the last German troops capable of retreating along the Warsaw highway over the Vistula at Siedlce, assisted by the *Luftwaffe*'s crack *Hermann Goering* Division. At the beginning of August, the *Totenkopf* was joined by *Wiking*, just as the Polish Home Army rose in Warsaw.

The *SS Panzer* divisions did not take part in the ruthless crushing of the Warsaw uprising, the brutal fight being left to two of the most violent units in the *SS*, the *Dirlewanger* and *Kaminski* Brigades, whilst the two *SS* divisions together with *Herman Goering* and the 4th

LEFT: Troops of the 4th *SS-Polizei* Division strap an injured soldier to the sidecar of a motorcycle combination during the division's withdrawal in Army Group North sector. During the course of this massive Red Army offensive, two *Waffen-SS Panzer* Divisions were caught in these traps: *Wiking* in the Cherkassy Pocket and the *Leibstandarte*, along with 2500 troops from the *Kampfgruppe Das Reich*, in the south.

and 19th *Panzer* Divisions saw extensive action northeast of Warsaw.

The fighting withdrawal had been a gruelling battle of attrition for those German divisions that had managed to escape from the Russian slaughter. Fortunately for the surviving German forces, the Soviet offensive had now run out of momentum. The Red Army's troops were too exhausted, and their vehicles were in great need of maintenance and repair.

But the lull in Poland was not mirrored elsewhere. In mid-July, another massive offensive was launched by the Soviet Ukrainian Fronts. On 20 August, Malinovsky's 2nd Ukrainian Front broke through powerful German defences, and the Red Army reached the Bulgarian border on 1 September. Within a week, Soviet troops reached the Yugoslav frontier. On 8 September, Bulgaria and Romania then declared war on Germany. On 23 September, Soviet forces arrived on the Hungarian border and immediately raced through the country for the Danube, finally reaching the river to the south of Budapest.

Hitler placed the utmost importance on the defence of Hungary. Against all military logic, he felt that it was Hungary and not the Vistula River which presented a natural barrier against an advance upon Berlin. He soon issued orders that

his premier divisions, including the *Waffen-SS* forces positioned along the Vistula should be transferred to Hungary. Reinforcements were provided by Army Groups E and F, withdrawing fron Greece and the Balkans.

The Germans had established a very strong defensive position southwest of the city of Budapest, and in order to bolster the defence of the Hungarian capital the VI *SS Panzer* Corps, comprising the 3rd *SS Panzer* Division *Totenkopf* and the 5th *SS Panzer* Division *Wiking*, were transferred from the Warsaw area. The defence of Budapest also included the 8th *SS Kavallerie* Division *Florian Geyer*, 22nd *SS Freiwilligen-Kavallerie* Division *Maria Theresia* and 18th *SS Freiwilligen-Panzergrenadier* Division *Horst Wessel*. The garrison fought for two solid months until it fell on 11 February 1945, when some 30,000 of the surviving defenders tried to break out to the west.

The surrender of Budapest meant that a large number of Russian formations were released to join a new offensive against the German Army. Although resistance by both the *Wehrmacht* and *Waffen-SS* was fierce, they were still unable to contain the Red juggernaut. Thus they were forced to continue their fighting withdrawal – at crippling cost.

ABOVE: The crew of a Tiger tank take a break in a Russian village early in 1944. *Das Reich, Totenkopf* and *Leibstandarte* all operated closely with the heavy *SS Panzer* companies who controlled the massive war machines. Slow and unreliable, they were nevertheless immensely powerful, and in the hands of an expert could be devastating. One such expert was the ace of all tank aces, *SS Obersturmführer* Michael Wittmann. Fighting on the edge of the Pripet Marshes,

Wittmann's Tiger with two others surprised and destroyed an entire Soviet tank group. Five days later, on 14 January Wittmann fought another mass of Soviet armoured vehicles. During seven hours of combat, Wittman manoeuvred aggressively through poor visibility, and by the end of the battle had smashed no less than 16 Red tanks. By the end of the day, a further three tanks and three super-heavy SP guns had also fallen victim to his lethal Tigers.

LEFT: In Army Group North during the 4th *SS-Polizei* Division's withdrawal in early 1944, an officer gives the Nazi salute to his commanding officer as he departs back to his divisional headquarters. As the Red Army gathered strength in the northern sector of the Front, *Waffen-SS* foreign legions were deployed to the Baltic region to confront this developing threat. Commanded by one of the toughest commanders in the SS, Felix Steiner, the III *SS Panzer* Corps included the 11th *SS Panzergrenadier* Division *Nordland* and *SS* Brigade *Nederland*. Steiner had been instrumental in the original creation of the *Waffen-SS*.

ABOVE: Members of an *SS* maintenance company work on an *SS* Tiger in the field. Due to its heavy armour, the Tiger was more resistant to combat damage than other tanks. As a result, the maintenance companies were often able to repair Tigers at the front, instead of wasting valuable time recovering and transferring them to specialized workshops, usually located many miles from the front lines. The Tiger's biggest failing was its lack of mobility: it was slow, and its 700 bhp Maybach engine consumed almost 3 litres (5$^{1}/_{4}$ pints) of fuel for each kilometre ($^{2}/_{3}$ mile) on the road, rising to 5 litres (8$^{3}/_{4}$ pints) when travelling cross-country. But in the right terrain, its powerful 8.8cm (3.45in) cannon could dominate a battlefield.

ABOVE: Troops take cover behind two Tiger tanks during heavy fighting in the Cherkassy Pocket in February 1944. Movement for the retreating German forces over the thawing ice was very difficult, and the Red Army took full advantage of the situation by launching murderous barrages of artillery and rocket fire. The *SS Sturmbrigade Wallonie* suffered terrible losses, with more than 70 per cent of its strength destroyed. In order to prevent total destruction, the

*Wiking* Division turned back the few remaining *Panzers* it had scraped together and held off the enemy just long enough to allow the breakout troops to reach the German lines. It was what was becoming a typical *Waffen-SS* self-sacrifice – the rear guard was overrun and wiped out. In total, some 32,000 German soldiers escaped almost certain slaughter inside the Cherkassy Pocket, and their survival was mostly due to the stubborn defence by the *SS Wiking* Division.

LEFT: *SS Panzergrenadiers* hitching a lift onboard Tiger tanks in early 1944. The tanks have all received a coating of *Zimmerit* anti-magnetic mine paste. The Tiger tank saw extensive action on the Eastern Front, first appearing outside Leningrad in November 1942. It was operated by the *Schwere Panzer Kompanien* of the *SS* divisions, which had nine Tigers in each of the three *SS Panzer* Regiments. Three semi-independent heavy *Abteilungen* were also created, attached at corps level. At the end of the war, the nominal strength (rarely achieved) of a heavy *Panzer Abteilung* was roughly 44 tanks and 900 men. Each unit was subdivided into 3 companies of 14 tanks each, plus two *Abteilung* command tanks.

ABOVE: Passing through a destroyed town, an Sd.Kfz 250 light armoured half-track carries grenadiers on the way to the front. The weight of this troop-carrying variant was 5.3 tonnes. It could carry a 1-tonne payload and could reach a top speed of 60kph (37mph). By 1943, the Sd.Kfz 250 was increasingly at the forefront of combat and consequently the Germans developed a range of models to suit the needs of the soldier in battle. The basic Sd.Kfz 250/1 was mainly issued to armoured reconnaissance and engineer companies. The Sd.Kfz 250/3 *leichter Funkpanzerwagen* radio vehicle was a command half-track and carried the frame aerial. The later Sd.Kfz 250/3 variant, however, featured a pole and star aerial in place of the frame aerial. The Sd.Kfz 250/7 was primarily used in a combat role and had a dedicated mortar carrier. The Sd.Kfz 250/8 was armed with a potent 7.5cm (2.95in) KwK L/24 gun, and mounted above this main armament was a 7.92cm (3.1in) MG 42 machine gun. Over 7000 vehicles were built by Büssing-NAG, Weserhütte, Wumag, Wegmann, Ritscher and Deutsche Werk between 1939 and 1945.

LEFT: A *Leibstandarte* MG 34 machine gun crew dressed snugly in their white camouflage smocks passes through an abandoned Russian trench early in 1944. Behind the men are two knocked-out T-34 tanks. On 24 January 1944, the *Leibstandarte* Division spearheaded an attack from the Vinnitsa area against the Russian First Tank Army, which had driven at speed across the Bug River. Four days later, they led the First *Panzer* Army's own envelopment of a Soviet pincer movement. The XLVI and the III Corps cast a net, which trapped a number of Soviet divisions. More than 700 tanks and self-propelled guns as well as 8000 prisoners were captured. However it was only a temporary triumph; constant heavy fighting and combat losses meant that by 28 February, the division's operational strength was just three tanks and four self-propelled guns!

ABOVE: Spread across the frozen Cherkassy steppe, a Pz.Kpfw.IV, a Panther and a number of Sd.Kfz 251 half-tracks, probably from III *Panzer* Corps, can be seen in action. Almost 50,000 German troops were trapped around Svenegordka. Requests to allow them to break out were refused by Hitler, who demanded that the Dnieper line be held at all costs. Elaborate and unrealistic plans were drawn up for a breakthrough, to be followed by a defeat of the encircling Russian divisions and the recapture of Kiev. Early in February 1944, the 1st *Panzer* and the *Leibstandarte* Divisions were ordered into attack. The *Leibstandarte* drove an armoured wedge deep into the Soviet front, but the offensive quickly turned into a retreat as the *Panzers* fought yard by yard to wrench open a gap through which the forces trapped in the pocket could escape.

ABOVE: The Tiger had two out of the three key assets of an armoured vehicle. Although far from mobile, it had excellent firepower thanks to its lethal 8.8cm (3.45in) gun, and its thick frontal armour meant that it was the best protected tank of its time. Even its side armour was thick enough to neutralize the threat of any but the largest of Allied anti-tank guns at normal combat ranges. *Waffen-SS* tank crews appreciated that its battlefield survivability was far greater than that of the widely-used Pz.Kpfw.IV. Outnumbered Tiger crews often fought off determined attacks by much larger enemy forces, so it quickly gained an awesome reputation. The psychological impact of this massive tank also proved an asset to the Tiger crews. However, they were expensive and difficult both to build and maintain, so there were never enough of them.

ABOVE: A rare photograph showing soldiers belonging to *Kampfgruppe Das Reich* moving along a trench in January 1944. Just weeks before, the Russians had unleashed their winter offensive and were driving German formations westward. The withdrawal continued through deep snowdrifts and in the face of terrible blizzards. The Russian offensive hit the *Kampfgruppe* hard, and its fighting retreat continued with ever-increasing casualties. During the day, units dug in and tried with some degree of success to fight off their attackers. By night they marched, but they could not cover the impressive distances achieved in the summer. Supplies were dwindling, and in the harsh winter weather the men could not live off the land. Short rations meant that each soldier was weaker, and could not move as far or as fast.

LEFT: *Waffen-SS Panzergrenadiers* move into action alongside a StuG.III Ausf. G self-propelled gun, in early 1944. Despite the determined resistance put up by the *SS* during this period, losses in men and equipment continued to rise rapidly in the face of overwhelming Soviet force. The *Kampfgruppe Das Reich* saw extensive action as the Red Army continued to push westward and out of the Ukraine. By January 1944, the *Kampfgruppe* had lost more than 1000 of its 5000 soldiers. In March, the exhausted remnants of the unit had to carry on fighting its way through the Cherkassy Pocket before reaching relative safety at Buszacz, where they were under the protection of the armoured vehicles of the Fourth *Panzer* Army.

ABOVE: *Waffen-SS Panzergrenadiers* keep low to the snow as a small group of Tiger tanks moves forward across the frozen plain in the Cherkassy region in early 1944. When the *Leibstandarte* and First *Panzer* Army attacked the pocket on 8 February 1944, elements of the *SS* and 16th *Panzer* Divisions reached and established bridgeheads across the Gniloi Tickich River. Michael Wittmann's Tigers played a significant part in these assaults. The *SS* tank ace took 11 Tigers out on patrol, during which he destroyed nine T-34 tanks. Over the next days, he and the crews of the other Tigers in Wittmann's platoon continued to destroy Soviet vehicles. Wittmann himself raised his personal score to 107 enemy machines destroyed in several days of bitter combat. By the time he was transferred to France that spring, his score had risen to 117.

ABOVE: Soldiers of the *Kampfgruppe Das Reich* make their way through the snow. These men are part of an MG 42 machine gun crew. For days, the *Kampfgruppe* had been forced to fight on half rations. They moved by night, exhausted by fighting with too little food. Once at a new bivouac, they had to dig defensive positions ready to fight off further Soviet daylight attack. Losses were high – one battalion was only 60 per cent and another only 55 per cent mobile. What made matters worse was the fact that not a single replacement had been received. So badly were they suffering, that the high command had to downgrade the combat ability of the *Kampfgruppe*'s infantry component. It was high time that this elite formation was withdrawn and rested, before it was totally destroyed and it was sent to join the rest of *Das Reich* in France.

RIGHT: This typical *Waffen-SS* soldier is wearing an issue white camouflage smock and is armed with an MP 38/40 sub-machine gun. Because the smock was warm and was effective at keeping out the severe winds, while at the same time providing excellent camouflage in the snow, the *SS* men fighting in the east tended to wear the uniform day and night for weeks on end. Keeping warm was more important than personal hygiene. However, the white jackets and trousers picked up dirt with such extensive wear, and soon became filthy – defeating the object of the white camouflage. It was impossible to wash these garments in winter at the front, as the thick inner lining made it all but impossible for the uniform to dry out. As a partial solution to the problem, many combat troops were supplied with a thin, easily-washable cotton cover, cape or suit, which each soldier could use over his existing uniform and equipment.

ABOVE: On the southern front during the winter of 1944, an *SS* flak crew mans a 2cm (0.78in) *Flakvierling* 38 quadruple-barrelled anti-aircraft gun. This was designed to counter high-performance aircraft flying at low level; earlier single-barrel weapons became less effective as the war progressed. However, it was a fearsome weapon in ground combat. It had a maximum theoretical rate of fire of around 1900 rounds per minute, though in practice this was reduced to under 1000 rpm. An *SS* divisional *Flak abteilung* would usually include two batteries of four quadruple guns. Each complete Flakvierling 38 cost RM20,000. It became the most effective German light AA weapon, feared and respected by all low-flying Allied aircrews.

ABOVE: Tiger tanks accompanied by *SS Panzer-grenadiers* move across the frozen steppes of the Ukraine early in 1944. In the face of stiff Red Army opposition, the first four months of the year were characterized by a series of withdrawals from one natural barrier to another. The Red Army was so powerful that even the best of the *Waffen-SS* divisions could not slow the advance enough to effect the situation decisively. Even the mighty *SS* Tigers could be vulnerable to the powerful Soviet SU-152 assault gun, nicknamed the 'Beast Hunter' by Russian soldiers because its chosen prey were the *Wehrmacht*'s Panthers and Tigers.

BELOW: *Panzergrenadiers* hitch a lift on board a Panther during operations on the southern front early in 1944. The main opponent of the Panther in 1944 was the T-34/85, which was not as well armoured and had a slightly less-powerful gun than the German machine's 7.5cm (2.95in) KwK42 L/70 gun. However, by this time the Soviet tank was being built in huge numbers, 10 being completed for every example of the much more complex Panther which entered service. This photograph was probably taken during operations by *Panzer* Regiment 11 of 6th *Panzer* Division, which was given the task of spearheading the attack to relieve the Cherkassy Pocket.

LEFT: *SS* troops in a captured Russian trench during the early months of 1944. A knocked-out T-34 tank has been dug in to the side of the trench to act as a fixed anti-tank position. Improvised fortifications like these often presented formidable obstacles to the Germans during their advance. However, by 1944 the *Wehrmacht's* exhausted formations were in full retreat, so its soldiers rarely encountered the extensive lines of steel and concrete defences which had characterized Soviet positions when they were on the defensive. The Germans took a leaf from the Soviet book in the last years of the war, mounting tank turrets in fixed defensive points during the final stages of the fighting on the Eastern Front.

ABOVE: A Tiger crew loading shells through the hatch of a Tiger tank in the Cherkassy Pocket early in 1944. The only reasonably intact German formation available to help relieve the German forces trapped inside the pocket was Hermann Breith's III *Panzer* Corps, comprising the *Leibstandarte*, 16th and 17th *Panzer* Divisions and the Heavy *Panzer* Regiment *Bäke*, named after its commander, Lieutenant-Colonel Dr Franz Bäke. This regiment comprised one battalion of Tigers and one of Panthers. The only *Panzer*

division actually in the pocket was *Wiking*, and this was used to protect the left flank, while the *Walloon Brigade* formed the rearguard. Only 632 out of the 2000 *Walloon* volunteers trapped in the pocket would survive. The terrible weather conditions meant that all the artillery had to be abandoned, because it was impossible to tow the heavy guns through the ice, water and mud. What was worse was that most of the wounded had to be left behind as well, tended by volunteers from the medical staff.

**ABOVE:** *SS* infantry help clear a route through the snow to provide a passage for a group of Pz.Kpfw.IV Ausf. H in March 1944. The deep snow had the same effect as mud on a tracked armoured vehicle and could quite easily immobilize it until it could be dug free. The Pz.Kpfw.IV was now nearing obsolescence, but it could still be effective on the battlefield. The *Panzer* IVs of the *SS Panzer* Division *Wiking* proved to be

invaluable during the bloody battle in the Cherkassy Pocket. *SS Untersturmführer* Kurt Schumacher won the Knight's Cross for his outstanding bravery whilst commanding a Pz.Kpfw.IV. Singlehandedly this *Panzer* ace and his crew destroyed eight T-34 tanks in one battle. Two days later he was even more successful, when he engaged a Russian enemy tank company, destroying another 13 armoured vehicles.

**LEFT:** Early 1944, and a Pz.Kpfw.III rolls along a frozen road in southern Russia before engaging strong enemy units. By this period of the war, the *Waffen-SS* retained only a handful of Panzer IIIs. The vehicle had been the mainstay of Germany's *Panzer* divisions early in the war, but it was now seriously outgunned by most Allied tanks. By late 1944, the Germans had relegated virtually all of them to training units, though the assault guns and artillery pieces based on the same chassis remained effective. However, as the Soviet Army thundered through the Baltic states at the end of the year, an *SS Panzer* brigade was quickly raised, which included five old Pz.Kpfw.III tanks. Named *SS Panzer Brigade Gross*, it saw action against Soviet armour on the northern sector of the Eastern Front.

LEFT: *SS Panzergrenadiers* march across the snow in the wake of a Tiger tank. Note the bayonet attached to the grenadier's bolt-action rifle, suggesting that he anticipates close-quarter combat in the near future. By the winter of 1944, the *Waffen-SS* had taken on a decidedly defensive posture: the battle-field fanaticism of the indoctrinated *SS* men could not by itself offset the over-whelming inferiority of their numbers. Yet in spite of this, many of the members of the *SS* remained true believers in the *Führer*, long after the vast mass of the German population had come to accept that the war was lost.

ABOVE: It is early spring in 1944 and a *Waffen-SS* mortar crew take cover beside a main road in western Russia. Halted on the road is a column of camouflaged Marder III self-propelled light tank destroyers. Based on the chassis of a Czech light tank, this vehicle weighed 10.5 tonnes and was armed with a 7.5cm (2.95in) Pak 40/3 L/46 gun. The Marder III proved to be an effective weapon and provided *Waffen-SS* grenadiers with the mobile anti-tank capability they so desperately needed. It continued serving in frontline *SS* divisions until late in the war, alongside the *Jagdpanzer* 38(t) tank killer based on the same Czech chassis.

RIGHT: February 1944, and an *SS* flak crew prepare for action with a 3.7cm (1.45in) self-propelled anti-aircraft gun mounted on an Sd.Kfz 7/2 half-track. Introduced to replace the 2cm (0.78in) flak guns that dated from the 1930s, it was also effective against lightly armoured ground targets. During the withdrawal, *Waffen-SS* and *Wehrmacht* divisions lost those vehicles destroyed in combat and those damaged ones which could not be repaired in time. Lack of transport meant that artillery pieces had to be abandoned. Artillery crews were ordered to fire all their remaining ammunition, then retreat.

ABOVE: A *Waffen-SS* machine gunner in a defensive position in the snow. Although the MG 34 seen here had been supplanted by the faster-firing MG 42, it was still an effective weapon and was used until the end of the war. By 1944, the *Waffen-SS* had changed greatly from the select group of men who had marched victoriously through France in 1940: now, with the military reverses on the Eastern Front in full swing, the *SS* had become a racially heterogeneous organization of one million men recruited from all over Europe. Even the *Leibstandarte*, *Das Reich* and *Hitlerjugend* divisions had non-German members by 1944.

# LAST BATTLES

The principle objective of the Red Army in January 1945 was Berlin, but the Soviet Winter Offensive broke out all along the Eastern Front from the Baltic to the Carpathians.

In the north, an assault along the Baltic coast was aimed at crushing those German units which were all that remained of the once mighty Army Group North. Hitler refused to allow the evacuation of 20 divisions – half a million men – which had been bypassed in the Kurland peninsula. These heavy attacks eventually cut the vast territory formerly occupied by Germany in the northeast to a few small pockets of land surrounding three ports: Libau in Kurland, Pillau in East Prussia and Danzig at the mouth of the Vistula. Here along the Baltic German defenders were reorganized as Army Group Centre in East Prussia and Army Group Kurland, the former Army Group North. Each *Wehrmacht* and

LEFT: Cold and weary *Waffen-SS* men near the city of Narva in Estonia in February 1944. Inside the city, soldiers of the *Nordland* and *Nederland* Divisions fought a bloody battle of attrition in the rubble-strewn streets. While the battle for Narva raged, the Soviets tried to outflank the city by making a landing on the coast west of the city. The landing force was engaged and destroyed by the Latvian *SS-Freiwilliges* brigade, which later became the 19th *Waffen Grenadier* Division *der SS (lettische Nr. 2)*.

*Waffen-SS* soldier defending these areas was aware of the significance of being overrun. Not only would the coastal garrisons there be cut off and eventually destroyed, but this would also prevent the masses of civilian refugees from escaping from those ports.

However, the Germans forces were fighting against a vastly superior force. The Russians had more than twice the number of infantry, nearly four times as much armour, seven times the artillery and an air force six times larger than could be deployed by the *Luftwaffe*. All the German formations were understrength, and their defensive capabilities depended greatly on the old Prussian and Silesian border fortresses of Breslau, Stettin, Küstrin, Folburg, Insterburg and Königsberg.

Big though the Soviet force in the Baltic was, it was a sideshow compared to the forces available to the Red Army further south. There, the winter offensive was to be a massive two-pronged attack through Poland, one leading along the Warsaw–Berlin axis commanded by Zhukov, with the other for Breslau under the command of General Konev. On 12 January 1945, Konev's offensive began with his 1st Ukrainian Front making deep penetrating drives against German defences. On the first day, its brutal and terrifying advance smashed through the Fourth *Panzer* Army to a depth of more than 32km (20 miles). Krakow was immediately threatened and German forces were quickly manoeuvred to defend this once great Polish fortress city.

Zhukov's 1st Belorussian Front began its drive along the Warsaw–Berlin axis on 14 January, striking out from the Vistula south of Warsaw. The city was quickly encircled and it fell three days later. In quick succession, Rokossovsky's 2nd Belorussian, Chernyakovsky's 3rd Belorussian, Bagramyan's 1st Baltic and Yeremenko's 2nd Baltic Fronts joined in.

In an attempt to at least delay the massive Red Army war machine in its progress towards the German capital, Berlin, Josef 'Sepp' Dietrich's Sixth *SS Panzer* Army was withdrawn from the failing Ardennes campaign in the west and was ordered eastwards.

On 20 January, Hitler announced to his dumbfounded commanders that he would not use the Sixth *SS Panzer* Army for defensive purposes in Poland against Zhukov's forces. Instead, he revealed, 'I'm going to attack the Russians where they least expect it. The Sixth *SS Panzer* Army is off to Budapest! If we start an offensive in Hungary, the Russians will have to go too.' Hitler's wild diversionary tactic of sending this elite *SS Panzer* Army to Hungary did nothing to impede the Red Army's drive through Poland. As events proved, the 2nd, 3rd and 4th Ukrainian fronts could deal quite adequately with the 6th *SS Panzer* army intervention in Hungary.

What forces were available to try and stem the Red Army's advance to the frontiers of the *Reich* were pulled together into a new army group, 'Army Group Vistula', under the command of

---

## Himmler was unfit to lead an army. Blundering incompetence in commanding Army Group Vistula earned him the contempt of many of his battle-hardened *Waffen-SS* troops.

---

*Reichsführer-SS* Heinrich Himmler. Army Group Vistula was positioned behind the threatened front and consisted mainly of *Volkssturm* units and militia groups too young or too old to serve in the regular Army. Along this weak front, a number of volunteer *SS* units bolstered the understrength and under-trained forces, but they too had little with which to impede the Russian onslaught, apart from courage.

In the days that followed, there was a massive stampede westwards of refugees, leaving their farms, villages and towns in a frantic attempt to escape from the clutches of the Red Army.

Nothing could prevent the Soviet advance. The city of Memel fell on 27 January, Thorn two weeks later, and on 22 February Poznan was

RIGHT: *SS Panzer-grenadiers* dug in during vicious fighting in the Narva region in February 1944. The soldier is armed with an MG 34 machine gun. The city of Narva, about 140km (85 miles) west along the Gulf of Finland from Leningrad, was the gateway to Estonia. The Germans established a strong defensive position along the west bank of the River Narva. During February and March 1944, grenadiers belong-ing to the *SS-Nordland* and *SS-Nederland* Divisions also dug in east of the city, covering a large area of territory on the approaches to Narva. They would hold out until late July, when they were forced back to the west bank. The Germans evacuated the city on 25 July and over the next three months fell back through Estonia and Latvia to Courland, where they were trapped.

captured. Küstrin held out until 29 March, and the city of Königsberg until mid-April.

The besieged fortress city of Breslau held out until the end of the war. A motley collection of *SS* soldiers, *Volkssturm* and *Hitlerjugend* had fought in the rubble-strewn streets with no prospect of survival. Almost 60,000 Soviet soldiers had been killed or wounded trying to capture it, with the loss of some 29,000 German military and civilian casualties.

As German forces continued to fall back, they tried frantically to prevent the Red Army from bursting through to capture Berlin, the capital of the *Reich*. Every day they held the Soviets back was another day of survival for those at the heart of the Fatherland.

The forces defending the Reich were often called divisions, but they were no more than shards and splinters simply thrown together to defend the frontiers of Germany. What was left of the *Wehrmacht*, *Volkssturm*, *Hitlerjugend* and *Waffen-SS* were now defending their homeland against a pitiless foe that had every cause to hate Hitler and his 'Thousand Year Reich.'

ABOVE: A rare photograph showing *Waffen-SS* foreign volunteers withdrawing from Army Group North. As the Red Army approached the Baltic States, all able-bodied men of Estonia and Latvia were subjected to conscription into Latvian and Estonian *Waffen-SS* grenadier divisions. On the northern sector of the Russian front, the Norwegian Legion was disbanded, and veterans who had survived more than two years on the Russian plains were encouraged to volunteer, some to have *Waffen-SS* status in the 1st Battalion of the 2nd *SS-Norge* Regiment. Survivors of the *Flanders* and *Nederland* Legions were also disbanded and the men joined the similar units of the *SS*. By 1944, foreign volunteers from all over Europe were serving in the *SS* legions, which ultimately made up half of the *Waffen-SS*.

LEFT: *Waffen-SS* volunteers trudging westward through the snow towards Estonia and Latvia. The main *Waffen-SS* force in this area was III *Panzer* Corps, commanded by *SS Gruppenführer* Felix Steiner, with the 11th *SS-Freiwilligen* Brigade *Nederland* and the *SS-Freiwilligen* Division *Nordland*. Within these two *SS* units were to be found Swiss, French, Finnish, Swedish, Danish and Dutch volunteers. Also in the region were other *SS* formations, like the 15th and 19th *Waffengrenadier* Divisions from Latvia, the 20th *Waffengrenadier* Division from Estonia, and the Flemish *Langemarck* Brigade and the Walloon *Sturmbrigade Wallonie*.

ABOVE: Men of the 4th *SS-Grenadier* Division *Polizei* seen while serving with Army Group North. Transferred to the Eastern Front in 1941, it had seen extensive operations in the north. Although the division proved its worth fighting for the Luga bridge-head, with the loss of over 2000 soldiers in bloody frontal assaults, it was not until January 1942 that it was given official *Waffen-SS* status. As a fully fledged *Waffen-SS* division it fought a series of battles along the Wolchow River. The following year, it saw action south of Ladoga and was upgraded to *Panzergrenadier* status. In March 1944, it was sent to Salonika to calm Bulgarian fears of an Allied invasion. It then became part of the 'Salonika–Aegean Administrative Area' with the Bulgarian 7th Infantry Division under the German LXXXI Army Corps.

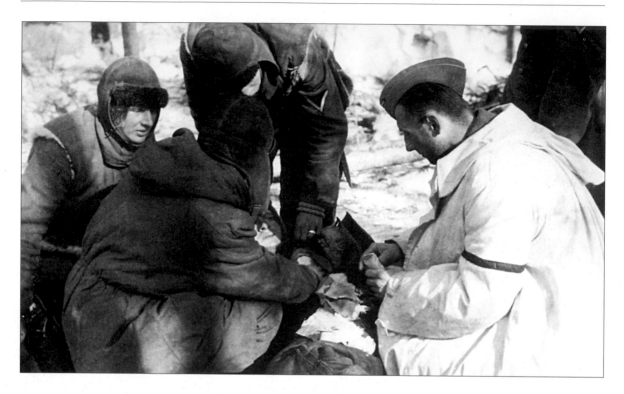

**ABOVE:** Members of the 4th *SS-Panzergrenadier* Division *Polizei* assist an injured comrade onto a stretcher. In August 1944, after operations in the Balkans, part of the division went to Bucharest while the remainder moved north to the Danzig area, then on to Pomerania, where it once again saw action.

Elements of the 4th *SS* were transported back to Danzig, where they became trapped by overwhelming Russian forces. Following a futile and costly battle of attrition that nearly destroyed the division, the remnants were moved across the Hela Peninsula and then shipped to Swinemunde.

**LEFT:** *Waffen-SS* men examine a knocked-out Russian T-26 light tank during heavy fighting in the winter of 1944. Based on a British Vickers design of the 1920s, this was the most common tank in the Soviet inventory at the outbreak of war. However, thousands were destroyed during Operation *Barbarossa* in the summer of 1941. Designed to provide close-support to infantry, each Soviet motor rifle division had one company of these vehicles. No match for a German *Panzer* IV, let alone the Panther which was the standard German *Panzer* in late 1944 and 1945, it was a comparatively rare sight by the time this photograph was taken.

ABOVE: An *SS* anti-tank crew commander scans the winter terrain for any signs of the approaching Russians. The weapon is a 3.7cm (1.45in) Pak, the standard German anti-tank gun at the outbreak of war. Long superseded by heavier weapons, it was still useful against softskin and light armoured vehicles.

The crew has draped white sheeting over the weapon to help it blend in with the surrounding terrain. This type of cheap but effective camouflage was used throughout the war, especially by 1944, when many troops did not have the time or resources to whitewash their weapons and vehicles.

ABOVE: *SS* infantry take to a shelter as an air raid warning sounds. By 1944, the Soviet Air Force was technically equal to that of the *Luftwaffe*, having brilliantly engineered simple-but-effective fighters and ground-attack aircraft. More to the point, they vastly outnumbered the *Luftwaffe*. On the ground, too, the Germans were faced with Red Army combat units that were well trained and had the latest equipment. The latest T-34 tank, for example, with its up-gunned 8.5cm (3.34in) main armament, and the new Josef Stalin heavy tank, armed with a 12.2cm (4.8in) gun, were a good match for the German Panther and Tiger.

ABOVE: An *SS* unit withdraws across a frozen river on the southern front early in 1944. By February, *SS Panzer* crews were in a mood of near desperation as their flight west was hindered by ice, snow or heavy mud. The situation had become so bad in some sectors that fuel and ammunition were unable to get through. The tank crews were forced to carry fuel to the front in buckets. With the spring thaw, many men slogged through knee-deep mud barefoot, finding this less

exhausting than having to stop and retrieve their boots every few metres. They also had severe problems withdrawing tracked and untracked vehicles together with horse-drawn wagons from a threatened sector. Wounded soldiers also proved a major handicap, but they could not be left to the less than tender mercies of the vengeful Red Army. Massive traffic jams continued to exacerbate the logistical nightmare of moving a defeated army westward.

RIGHT: *Waffen-SS Panzergrenadiers* mounted on Sd.Kfz. 251 halftracks withdraw through a village in western Russia. Some of the men can be seen wearing the fur-lined *SS* winter combat anorak, which was normally worn with winter trousers. By the spring of 1944, German strategy faced its ultimate challenge in the East. To the soldiers retreating across a land they had dominated since 1941, it had become a grim battle for survival. By this time, *Wehrmacht* and *Waffen-SS* strength in the east reached a new low of just 2,242,649 men, against some 6,077,000 Soviet soldiers. Even the elite *SS* formations had been starved of men and equipment to prepare for the long-expected Allied landings in the West.

ABOVE: A mountain trooper of the 6th *SS-Gebirgs* Division *Nord* attempts to keep his hands warm so that he can fire his Kar 98k rifle at a moment's notice. For a soldier defending a position without moving, the cold was a nightmare: numbness would creep inwards from extremities until the whole body was an aching mass of misery. Yet they were still required to react instantly to enemy actions. Hands and feet were not the only worries, however. Every man prayed that his rifle or machine gun would function properly when called upon. All had experienced or seen incidents where the cold had been intense enough to make metal brittle: amongst the first parts to fail were firing pins, snapping and rendering the weapons useless. In really cold weather, where the temperature dropped below -30°C (-22°F), mechanical parts would freeze solid.

ABOVE: *SS Nebeltruppe* adding foliage to their 15cm (5.9in) *Nebelwerfer* 41. This photograph was taken during the opening phases of Operation Bagration. On the morning of 22 June 1944, the third anniversary of the German invasion of Russia, the offensive against Army Group Centre began. The First Baltic and Third Belorussian Fronts attacked northwest and southwest of Vitebsk. The overwhelming strength of the Soviet assault shattered Army Group Centre and tore a

massive 320km (200-mile) gap in the bombed and blasted German front. On 13 July, the Soviet forces mounted an attack against Army Group North, while a further massive assault was made through the Ukraine. The German front in the east was ripped apart. By the end of July, Army Group Centre had been destroyed. The Red Army stood at the Gulf of Riga in the north, in the suburbs of Warsaw in the centre, and on the line of the San River in the Ukraine.

LEFT: SS and *Wehrmacht* panzergrenadiers take a break from the fighting in Poland in late October 1944. Four of the men are sitting on the tank wheels of a late variant Pz.Kpfw.IV. An Sd.Kfz. 251 half-track command vehicle can be seen parked nearby. Curiously, the Red Army seemed in no hurry to try to take Warsaw, and such assaults across the Vistula that were made were held off by the *Totenkopf*, *Wiking* and 19th *Panzer* Divisions. Part of the reason for Soviet inactivity was fatigue: they had advanced some 725km (450 miles) in just five weeks and had over-extended communications and supply lines. Stalin may also have been waiting for the Germans to put down the Warsaw Rising: the destruction of the Polish Home Army meant that the Soviets would be able to set up their own communist government when they eventually took the city.

ABOVE: Troops of the 6th *SS-Gebirgs* Division *Nord* stand watch in a trench. The soldier on the left is wearing a sheepskin coat and is armed with a Kar 98K rifle and a stick grenade. This *SS* mountain division remained in the far north of the Eastern Front until late 1944, when Finland signed an armistice with the USSR. *Nord* was withdrawn through Norway and shipped to Denmark. Here it joined depleted *ad hoc Wehrmacht* units on the Western Front. As *SS-Kampfgruppe Nord*, it took part in the attack through the Vosges designed to take pressure off the rapidly failing German offensive in the Ardennes.

ABOVE: The crew of a 3.7cm (1.45in) anti-tank gun remain vigilant as a column of troops and armoured vehicles pour along a road through Poland. In late 1944, the Soviets in both Poland and East Prussia remained relatively quiet. From August 1944 until the end of the year, the Eastern Front between the Carpathians and the Baltic barely shifted at all. The Red Army could have possibly won the war in the east by 1944, but Stalin shifted the centre of gravity of the

Eastern Front to the Balkans, possibly with a view to setting the foundations for postwar Soviet control of the area. It seemed the whole German position in Southern Europe was on the point of disintegration. However, Hitler was determined that he was not going to allow the Soviets to conquer Hungary without a fight. He issued orders for *Wehrmacht* and *Waffen-SS* divisions preparing to defend the Vistula to be transported to Hungary instead.

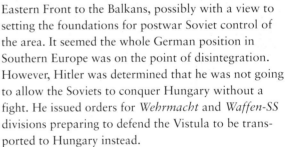

LEFT: A mixed group of *SS* and *Wehrmacht* troops move along a muddy road near the Vistula early in December 1944. Note the half-track towing a Pak 40. Strength comparisons on the Eastern Front showed that against 160 German units of between brigade and division size the Red Army fielded an astonishing 414 units at the front, 216 in front reserves, and 219 in reserves in depth. Against Army Group Centre, the 2nd and 3rd Belorussian Fronts could muster 1,670,000 men, 28,000 artillery pieces and mortars, and 3300 tanks and self-propelled artillery. Against Army Group A, the 1st Belorussian and 1st Ukrainian Fronts had a total of 2,200,000 troops, 6400 tanks and self-propelled artillery, and 46,000 artillery pieces.

RIGHT: A battery of StuG.III assault guns halt on a road to the west of Budapest in early February 1945, helpless as a mighty Soviet force tightens the noose around the Hungarian capital. On 29 January, the last attempt to relieve Budapest failed. Nevertheless, the beleaguered defenders, with no hope of rescue, refused to surrender and conducted a series of bitter battles in the rubble-strewn streets. From the original 50,000-man garrison, only 785 managed to claw their way out and reach the German lines. After the capture of Budapest, the Soviets increased the intensity of their offensive and began battering divisions of Army Group South. Taking the full brunt of the Soviet hammer blows were the *Totenkopf* and *Wiking* Divisions.

ABOVE: Seen early in 1945, a StuG.III Ausf. G assault gun together with a motorcycle combination cross a frozen field during operations in Hungary. It was on Boxing Day in 1944 that the Red Army completed the encirclement of Budapest. All through January, *Totenkopf* and *Wiking* tried to break through to the city, but they were too depleted and exhausted after months of continuous fighting to succeed. Slowly and systematically, the 50,000 or so German and Hungarian troops trapped in the Budapest pocket were compressed into a shrinking perimeter. It was not until early February 1945, when the IV *SS Panzer* Corps reluctantly abandoned its relief attempts, that the beleaguered troops inside the city tried to break out.

ABOVE: An *SS* flak gunner scours the Hungarian skies for Soviet aircraft. He is standing on the decking of an artillery tractor which mounts a 2cm (0.78in) *Flakvierling* 38 quadruple-barrelled anti-aircraft gun. Note the kill markings displayed on the gun shield. The Germans established a very strong defensive position southwest of the city of Budapest, designed to help bolster the defence of the Hungarian capital. Included in the German order of battle in the area was the VI *SS Panzer* Corps, which had among its units *Totenkopf*, *Wiking*, 8th *SS Kavallerie* Division *Florian Geyer*, 22nd *SS Freiwilligen Kavallerie* Division *Maria Theresia* and 18th *SS Freiwilligen Panzergrenadier* Division *Horst Wessel*.

ABOVE: A StuG.III Ausf. G in action. The vehicle has obviously seen some action as it has lost some of its side skirting. Note the smoke dischargers attached to the hull to the right of the gun mantlet. The vehicle commander is wearing the assault gun uniform and field grey M43 cap worn with the BeVo death's-head on the front and the eagle on the left side. The uniform was modelled on the black *SS Panzer* uniform. It was generally issued to self-propelled gun crews from summer of 1942. It was entirely made of field-grey cloth, and although all details of cut and design were the same as those for the black *Panzer* uniform, the insignia differed because the assault guns were part of the artillery and not part of the *Panzerwaffe*.

ABOVE: StuG.III assault guns are refuelled from the back of an Opel Blitz truck on a road to the west of Budapest. By this period of the war, Allied bombing had destroyed the greater part of Germany's synthetic oil plants and the fuel-starved *Wehrmacht* and *Waffen-SS* had become dependent on oil from the wells at Zisterdorf in Austria and around Lake Balaton in Hungary. Part of Hitler's preoccupation with Hungary was the fact that, if he did not keep control of these

important resources, his entire armoured force and what was left of the *Luftwaffe* would grind to a halt, and the war would be lost. It was to protect the oil-fields that Hitler made his last battlefield gamble, choosing to mount an offensive in Hungary with the Sixth *SS Panzer* Army, rather than retaining his elite formations along the River Oder in the defence of Berlin. He was convinced that his cherished *Waffen-SS* formations would yield him victory.

RIGHT: A *Nashorn* ('Rhinoceros') self-propelled anti-tank gun, mounting the deadly 8.8cm (3.45in) PaK 43/1 L/71 gun, fires at an enemy target during one the last Eastern Front battles of the war. The *Nashorn* was first introduced in time for the battle at Kursk in July 1943. It served with army and *SS schwere Panzerjager abteilungen*, and proved to be an effective mobile anti-tank weapon, well able to destroy Soviet heavy tanks at long ranges. Only 474 *Nashorns* and 20 of the similar *Hornisse* ('Hornet') were built. One drawback was its open-topped fighting compartment, and in 1944 it began to be replaced by the more heavily armoured *Jagdpanzer* IV and *Jagdpanther*. The *Nashorn* remained in service to the end of the war, however, providing a valuable long-range mobile anti-tank capability on all fronts.

LEFT: A *Nashorn* in action in Poland in 1945 uses a ruined building as cover. Tank hunters like the *Nashorn* engaged the enemy at long range. As early as 1941, the *Waffen-SS* had recognized that one of the weaknesses of its *Panzer* divisions was the serious lack of self-propelled artillery capable of keeping pace with the armoured spearheads. Initially the troops had to rely on the defensive power of conventional artillery along the front lines. But by 1942, effective self-propelled guns were entering service, ultimately becoming the the backbone of *SS* armoured artillery batteries until the very end of the war.

ABOVE: Caught on camera at the moment of firing is a battery of *Wespe* ('Wasp') self-propelled guns in defensive positions in southern Poland in late 1944. The *Wespe* and the heavier *Hummel* ('Bumble-Bee') formed the backbone of the *Panzer* artillery and served in armoured artillery battalions of both Army and *SS* *Panzer* divisions. The *Wespe* was armed with the standard 10.5cm (4.13in) light field howitzer in a thinly armoured, open-topped, boxed-like structure mounted on the chassis of a Pz.Kpfw.II tank. Ammunition stowage was limited to 32 rounds. The 10.5cm shells could be fired to a range of 4120m (4505yd).

ABOVE: As *Wehrmacht* and *Waffen-SS* forces were forced back down the narrowing funnel between the Baltic and the Carpathians, their command structure began to crumble. Each Red Army front now greatly exceeded any German army group in strength, and was vastly better supplied with ammunition and equipment. Here, an Sd.Kfz.2 *Kleines Kettenkraftrad* with driver and passenger moves along a very muddy road in February 1945. Built by NSU to a 1940 army order, the 'Kettenrad' was intended to serve as a lightweight tractor for use in difficult terrain. It proved to be an excellent performer in all conditions. Over 8340 were built, and the type saw service in every theatre. The vehicle could carry three men and could tow loads of up to half a ton – in this instance it is probably an ammunition trailer. Both the soldiers are wearing the field-grey *Einheitsfeldmütze* and the green splinter camouflage winter uniform.

# FALL OF THE REICH

**Despite the best efforts of the *Waffen-SS* to block the Red Army on the Eastern Front during the last months of the war, nothing could mask the fact that the Third Reich was doomed.**

The *Waffen-SS* was still growing at the end of 1944, but nothing could mask the fact that German arms were dwarfed by the superiority of the Red Army. It was estimated that the Russians had 6 million men along a front which stretched from the Adriatic to the Baltic. The great offensive that was to tear Germany in two began during the third week of January 1945. Marshal Konev's 1st Ukrainian Front surged into Silesia after the capture of Radom and Krakow.

On the night of 27 January, the German divisions of the 17th Army pulled out of the region and clawed their way back towards the River Oder. Fighting between the *SS* and the Red Army was merciless, with both sides instructing their men to stand where they were and fight to the death. In the German Army, those found

LEFT: A *Nashorn* self-propelled anti-tank gun in Poland in 1945. With its winter whitewash, it carries the name 'Tiger' on the side and an outlined national cross. The unit's emblem, a shield, is behind the open right rear access door, but is not clear enough to be identified. By this period of the war in the East, *Wehrmacht* and *Waffen-SS* were being driven back and drained of their resources. They were thus unable to sustain themselves in front of the Soviet onslaught.

guilty of malingering were hanged by the roadside without even a court martial. Those accused of desertion or of causing self-inflicted injuries were executed on the spot. Every day, soldiers would pass groups of freshly erected gallows where the SS had hanged deserters. Signs were tied around their necks, usually along the lines of, 'Here I hang because I did not believe in the *Führer*'.

With every defeat and withdrawal came an increasing pressure on unit commanders to impose harsher discipline on their weary, exhausted men. Conditions on the Eastern Front were miserable, not only for the newest *SS* recruits dragged from the Western Front to bolster the crumbling lines in the East, but also for the battle-hardened soldiers who had survived many months of bitter conflict against numerically superior forces.

Constantly digging in against never-ending artillery and air bombardment was a dispiriting experience. The cold, harsh weather during February and March 1945 prevented the *SS* soldiers from digging down very deeply, and living conditions there were similar to those their fathers had experienced in the trenches of World War I. All arms lacked experienced troops, numbers having been thinned drastically by the attrition of the previous year. German factories and transport infrastructure were also breaking down under the devastating attacks of British and American bombers. As a result, troops at the front were experiencing severe shortages of ammunition, fuel and vehicles. Some divisions issued instructions that key vehicles could be used only in an emergency, and battery fire was often prohibited without permission from the commanding officer. The average daily ration was two shells per gun.

As the great Red Army drive gathered momentum, more towns and villages fell. Suicidal opposition from a few *SS* strong points bypassed in earlier attacks often reduced the buildings and cobblestone streets they had been defending to burned and blasted rubble. Many isolated units spent days fighting a bloody defence. Russian soldiers frequently requested them to surrender and promised that no harm would come to them if they did so. But despite this assuring tone, most of the Germans were compelled to fight to the

death, for there were many *SS* men fanatically propping up the worn down *Wehrmacht* units.

As the Red Army advanced closer, life on the battlefield became much more depressing for the soldiers. Sitting in their squalid trenches, the faces of this once elite band of men became gaunt from the lack of sleep and their meagre diet. Most nights, they spent keeping their heads down, sheltering from the constant Soviet shelling. Nobody dared move during daylight hours. Not only did they fear Russian air attacks, but snipers took a heavy toll.

In Hungary, *Waffen-SS* troops continued fighting to stave off the ever-growing threat of being overrun. Despite the enemy's numerical superiority, the Sixth *SS Panzer* Army, made up

---

## Members of the best *Waffen-SS* units may have earned the right to call themselves soldiers like any others, but their fanaticism was far too often reflected in war crimes.

---

from the 1st *SS Panzer* Division *Leibstandarte*, 2nd *SS Panzer* Division *Das Reich*, 9th *SS Panzer* Division *Hohenstaufen* and the 12th *SS Hitlerjugend* Division, fought with their customary determination. In a number of places, *SS* soldiers managed to drive back the Russians up to 40km (25 miles).

However, when the Red Army launched its counteroffensive on 16 March 1945 along the entire sector west of Budapest, the *Waffen-SS* divisions struggled to maintain their front lines. In the confusion and mayhem that engulfed the battlefield, *Das Reich* desperately held open a corridor of escape for its men. By 25 March, the Russians had torn through the shattered German lines, forcing the best units of the once mighty *Waffen-SS* to withdraw or face total annihilation.

The army's commander, *SS-Oberstgruppenführer* 'Sepp' Dietrich, had in fact saved his *SS* men from ultimate catastrophe. However, back in

Berlin, Hitler angrily accused his most unswervingly loyal fighting band of cowardice and treachery and demanded the removal of the 'Adolf Hitler' cuff bands worn by the *Leibstandarte* as a punishment. Legend has it that Dietrich's troops were so insulted that they collected their decorations in a chamber pot, together with a limb of a dead comrade and sent them to Hitler.

By early April 1945 what was left of the *Waffen-SS* in Hungary had been driven into Austria. The bulk of the *SS* forces which now took up defensive positions around Vienna included remnants of *Wiking, Hohenstaufen, Totenkopf, Hitlerjugend*, and *Das Reich*. Overwhelmingly outnumbered, low on ammunition and food, they fought on until the remnants of their units were safely behind Allied lines and surrendered to the Americans.

Whilst most of the premier *Waffen-SS* divisions in the East were making a fighting withdrawal through Hungary and into Austria, European volunteer units in the central and northern sectors of the receding German front lines were thrown into battle in a desperate attempt to hold the Soviet advance. In these front lines were men of the French *SS-Charlemagne* Division, as well as Latvian, Dutch and Flemish *Waffen-SS* units.

In mid-April 1945, the Soviets successfully crossed the River Oder, sending General Heinrici's troops reeling back to the very edges of Berlin. In the south-eastern suburbs of the doomed city, exhausted and badly equipped Latvian, Norwegian and Danish *SS* soldiers, together with a few hundred survivors of the *SS Charlemagne* Division held the district around Tempelhof airport. But after heavy fighting in the area, they were driven from their weak positions and exposed to the horror of fighting an urban battle of attrition. Anti-communist and nationalist Russian volunteers of the 30th *Waffengrenadier* Division were transferred to General Andrei Vlassov's Free Russian Army. But within days, most had been killed or captured, which under the circumstances amounted to the same thing.

In other parts of Berlin, *Waffen-SS* soldiers were hard pressed to hold their weak positions. But Hitler, who lived in a fantasy world in the bunker beneath the Reich Chancellery, was determined to use his *SS* troops to save the crumbling capital. Troops under the command of *SS-Obergruppenführer* Felix Steiner were to attack immediately from their positions in the Eberswalde, on the flank of Manteuffel's Third *Panzer* Army; then they were to drive south, cutting off the Russian assault on Berlin. On Hitler's map, the plan looked brilliant. But it was impossible to gather the forces to make Army Group Steiner even remotely operational. The city was doomed.

Elsewhere on the Eastern Front, other *Waffen-SS* volunteer units were being systematically annihilated. The *Wiking* Division had been shredded in the fighting for the approaches to Vienna. The 14th *Waffengrenadier* Division *der SS* from the Ukraine surrendered to the Red Army in Czechoslovakia. Most of the survivors faced Stalin's vengeful wrath in the form of the Gulag or the firing squad. Near Prague, the Hungarian *SS* volunteers of the *Horst Wessel* division capitulated along with the Estonians of the 20th *Waffengrenadier* Division *der SS*. The *Maria Theresia* Division had been destroyed during the final battles for Budapest.

By late April 1945, the *Waffen-SS* was all but destroyed. As Hitler planned his suicide beneath the blitzed *Reich* Chancellery, he heaped abuse at his once vaunted bodyguard unit. In his eyes, they had failed. However, in the eyes of the *SS* soldiers, duty had not been ignored, and it was now possible to lay down their arms in the sound knowledge that no military formation in history had achieved more. They had battled across the vast expanses of the Soviet Union to the gates of Moscow. They had fought through appalling winter weather and made great advances during the summer offensive of 1942. They had shown their skill and endurance at Kharkov and Kursk, and gone on to protect the withdrawals of the rest of the German army.

Nobody could deny that these men, in their brief and extraordinary existence, had won a reputation for daring and professionalism in combat. But despite their great achievements, nothing could mask the fact that those achievements were also stained with the darkest hues of atrocity.

ABOVE: Mounted on an artillery tractor, a flak gun has been elevated into its firing position. Note the soldier with the tripod-mounted range finder. In clear weather this device was able to calculate the approximate height and distance of an aircraft by a series of grid references imposed on the field of view. Once determined, the information could then be quickly given to the flak crew who would aim and fire accordingly.

This photograph was taken days after Konev's 1st Ukrainian Front had unleashed its armour against the Fourth *Panzer* Army. Luckily for the Germans, the low-hanging clouds and mist had kept the bulk of the Soviet Air Force temporarily grounded. In January 1945, the Red Army had total air superiority in the East and could field some 10,000 aircraft against less than 1875 short-of-fuel *Luftwaffe* machines.

RIGHT: A soldier from an *SS* rocket launcher battalion secures the projectiles before firing the 15cm (5.9in) *Panzerwerfer* 42 rocket launcher. This photograph was taken during the offensive 'Spring Awakening' in early March 1945. This, the last German offensive of the war, was planned by Hitler to throw the Soviets back across the Danube, saving the precious Hungarian oil wells. The attack began in earnest at dawn on 6 March, and was mounted by the Sixth *SS Panzer* Army, Eighth Army, Sixth Army and the Hungarian Third Army. The weather was far from springlike. In fact, heavy snow made conditions even worse.

ABOVE: On 12 January 1945, a battery of *Wespe* 10.5cm (4.13in) leFH 18/2 L/28 self-propelled artillery guns are dug in along the front lines, ready to open fire against advancing units of Marshal Konev's 1st Ukrainian Front. This was the last winter offensive of the war. By the evening of the first day, Konev's armour had broken the front of the Fourth *Panzer* Army to a depth of some 32km (20 miles). Within two days, Zhukov's offensive on the Warsaw–Berlin axis began with even greater ferocity. Two weeks later, the Red Army had smashed its way through the desolation that was Poland, and had penetrated the frontiers of the Reich itself. It was obvious that the final offensive would be against Berlin, but the premier *Waffen-SS* divisions were not brought in to save the capital. Instead, they remained embroiled in Hungary, fighting around the doomed city of Budapest.

ABOVE: A *Luftwaffe* flak crew in Hungary supporting *Wehrmacht* and *Waffen-SS* troops during the 'Spring Awakening' offensive. To increase the element of surprise, soldiers moving to the front were dropped from their transports about 18km (12 miles) from their jump-off positions. They were compelled to cover the remaining distance by foot across the snow, in order to avoid detection by Soviet reconnaissance aircraft. This meant that by the time the troops arrived at their launch point, they were totally exhausted and very cold. What made matters worse was that the men did not arrive at their appointed area of attack in time. The artillery barrage had already started, and by the time the German units arrived to start their attack, the scale of the bombardment had alerted the Soviets to the impending offensive.

RIGHT: An Sd.Kfz. 251 half-track laden with *SS Panzergrenadiers* follows tracked and untracked armoured vehicles towards a burning Hungarian village. The offensive was so secret that *SS* commanders were not allowed to reconnoitre the areas in which their units would operate just in case it revealed their attack. All identifying insignia were also removed.

ABOVE: *Waffen-SS* troops of the Sixth *SS Panzer* Army move across the thawing terrain in Hungary just prior to Hitler's 'Spring Awakening' offensive. On the left is a half-track mounted 3.7cm (1.45in) anti-tank gun. On the right, an Opel Blitz truck is carrying supplies. The Sixth *SS Panzer* Army consisted of the *Leibstandarte*, *Das Reich*, *Hohenstaufen* and the *Hitlerjugend* divisions. All of these elite *SS* formations had newly

arrived from the Ardennes, but they were mere shadows of the powerful units they had once been. Exhausted and lacking sufficient armour, they were nonetheless a formidable force and were capable of stemming the Red Army, if only temporarily. One unintended effect of their deployment was to make the Soviets fight even harder: the ordinary Soviet soldier hated all Germans, but he hated the *SS* above all else.

RIGHT: Camouflaged late variant Sd.Kfz. 251 half-tracks take up positions next to a lake during defensive operations in 1945. In spite of the huge losses sustained by the *Waffen-SS* divisions in the East, even the hard-bitten veterans of these elite formations were beginning to doubt their *Führer*. After the defeat of the *SS* around Lake Balaton, the Red Army continued its onslaught west of Budapest. By 2 April, the Soviets had successfully reached the Neusiedler Lake, on the frontier between Hungary and Austria. Just two days later, the last vestiges of Hitler's once mighty *SS* were driven out of Hungary forever. Survivors of the *Waffen-SS* divisions that had fought in Hungary were withdrawn to Austria to defend Vienna – though it was clear that many units were actually retreating westwards to surrender to the Americans.

BELOW: An *SS Hummel* crew loading fuel on board their vehicle during operations in Hungary late in March 1945. During the German 'Spring Awakening' offensive, *SS Panzer* crews and *Panzergrenadiers* spent a lot of their time floundering through deep mud as the spring thaw began in earnest. As had happened so often in Russia, vehicles became bogged down in the mire, and for most the going was almost impossible. Not surprisingly, the German attack was reduced to a crawl and severe losses were sustained as a result.

Despite the massive difficulties, the *Waffen-SS* men yet again displayed their customary determination, and even managed to drive back the enemy in some sectors of the front – the I *SS Panzer* Corps, for instance, successfully advanced some 40km (25 miles). However, the II *SS Panzer* Corps fared less well and could only manage to penetrate about 8km (5 miles). By the time fresh Red Army units were brought to bear on the German offensive, even the *SS* had nowhere to go but back, and the final retreat began.

RIGHT: Supported by a *Grille* ('Bison') self-propelled gun, *Waffen-SS* troops hold a thin defensive line in Hungary late in March 1945. Coming into service during 1943, the *Grille* mounted the 15cm (5.9in) SIG 33 infantry gun on the well-proven chassis of the Czech *Panzer* 38(t). These powerful vehicles served on all fronts from 1943, assigned to the heavy infantry gun companies of *Panzergrenadier* regiments. By 25 March, the Russians had smashed a 100km (60 mile) hole in the German defences and inflicted massive losses. However, around Lake Balaton the Sixth *SS Panzer* Army and two *Panzer* Corps, including the 16th *SS Panzergrenadier* Division *Reichsführer-SS*, were committed to the last desperate battle in Hungary. Within ten days, they had been forced to retreat. Hitler was infuriated at this 'betrayal' by his elite *Waffen-SS* formations.

ABOVE: In total, some 500,000 foreigners served in the *SS* during World War II, but the bulk of them were not volunteers and very few were idealists. The largest group of non-German *SS* were eastern Europeans – Latvians, Estonians, Ukrainians, Bosnians, Croats, Serbs, Albanians, Hungarians, Romanians, Bulgarians, Russians, and *Volksdeutscher*, or ethnic Germans of Eastern Europe. None of the 30 or more *SS* divisions in existence by 1945 were composed entirely of native Germans, not even the *Leibstandarte*. Nineteen of the so-called divisions consisted largely of foreign personnel. Although this 'foreign legion' boosted *SS* numbers, they were not as well trained or equipped as the original *Waffen-SS* formations.

ABOVE: Troops belonging to a *Nebelwerfer* battalion prepare for action in Austria in April 1945. Each man carries a single 15cm (5.9in) rocket to the *Nebelwerfer* rocket launcher. Anything and everything in the way of weaponry was by now being thrown into the front lines against the Soviets. In the *SS* Army sector in Austria, *Panzergrenadiers* were so few in numbers that a continuous defensive line could not be held. Quartermaster and supply organizations had broken down completely. Most equipment could no longer be replaced. Fuel shortages, caused mostly by the combined Anglo/American bomber offensive, now threatened to bring the whole army to a standstill. Various improvised measures were implemented in order to form units from the shattered remains of surviving companies. Shortages were so bad that the Sixth *Panzer* Army had only a handful of operational tanks available on 10 April 1945.

ABOVE: Infantry are digging in to defend eastern Austria against overwhelming odds during the early days of April 1945. During this period, Tolbukin's 3rd Ukrainian Front had already surrounded the city of Vienna on three sides, and the Soviet commander was ready to launch the final attack on the city. The Sixth *SS Panzer* Army no longer had the power to hold back the Red Army. All that the remnants of its exhausted divisions could do was to delay the inevitable loss of the Danube bridges for as long as possible. The men of the *Das Reich* Division were given the task to defend the principle bridges. The fighting in this sector raged for nine gruelling days as the *SS* fought from street to street, building to building. There were even small actions in the sewers, where flamethrower units from both sides were used to horrifying effect.

LEFT: An Sd.Kfz. 251 half-track heads the withdrawal of a shattered army early in April 1945. What remained of the front lines during this time was, for the most part, inexperienced training units. More experienced soldiers observed that the Soviets were playing with them 'like a cat with a mouse'. Sitting in their trenches, all the men were waiting for a single thing – the order to 'hurry up and retreat'. Whenever the Soviets pressed closer, there was almost invariably panic among the men. Most of the time, when a platoon commander telephoned back to company headquarters appealing for retreat, there was no reply; the men at the front feared, with some justification, that the very commanders who told them to stand and fight had abandoned them.

ABOVE: Men from an *SS Panzer* division watch as their StuG.III assault gun is towed out of the mire by an *Opel Blitz* truck and another assault gun. During the last weeks of the war, shortages in men and armour had become critical. Even the once powerful Sixth *SS Panzer* Army had been severely weakened. A report in late March 1945 on the condition of the army stated: '1st *SS Panzer* Division had been burnt out and the remnants of the division is with Army HQ. 12th *SS* Division is severely weakened. Only remnants of 3rd *SS* Division remain. 6th *SS* Division is weakened. 2nd *SS* Division is of average strength, and only one infantry regiment, part of the artillery and pioneer battalion of the 356th Infantry Division is being rested.' It was left to these divisions – divisions in name only – to defend the borders and cities of Austria.

ABOVE: *SS* foreign volunteers keeping under cover to avoid being spotted by an advancing T-34 tank during the last bitter weeks on the Eastern Front in 1945. The war was now drawing to an inevitable conclusion, but even at this late stage a number of *SS* commanders complained bitterly that the foreign volunteer replacements they were being sent were mostly under-nourished and physically deficient. They also reported that there was a general 'tendency to be disobedient and evasive', and there were also numerous cases of cowardice in combat. However, the fear of losing the war forced Himmler to generally ignore the complaints and send the foreign volunteers to the front line anyway. It was hardly surprising that they lacked the motivation of earlier volunteers, since in many cases it had been a choice of 'volunteer or be shot'. That said, a number of foreign-manned units were indeed courageous under fire and fought with varying degrees of determination and élan, most were neither trained nor equipped to fight against the massive Soviet tank and artillery concentrations with which they were faced in the last stages of the war.

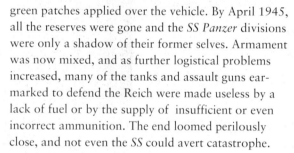

ABOVE: Two soldiers belonging to a *Luftwaffe Fallschirmjäger* unit are seen with *SS* troops in front of a stationary StuG.III Ausf. G self-propelled gun armed with an MG 34 machine gun. In their early days, the paratroopers had been a true elite, but by this late stage in the war their standards had slipped at least as far as those of the bulk of the *SS*. The self-propelled gun has intact hull side skirts and is painted in overall dark sand with a camouflage scheme of green patches applied over the vehicle. By April 1945, all the reserves were gone and the *SS Panzer* divisions were only a shadow of their former selves. Armament was now mixed, and as further logistical problems increased, many of the tanks and assault guns earmarked to defend the Reich were made useless by a lack of fuel or by the supply of insufficient or even incorrect ammunition. The end loomed perilously close, and not even the *SS* could avert catastrophe.

LEFT: A photograph showing the commander of a self-propelled gun in action during the last weeks of the war in the East. Heavy foliage has been applied over the vehicle in order to break up its distinctive outline. The thought of fighting on German soil for the first time resulted in mixed feelings among the men. Although the defence of the Reich automatically stirred the emotions, the general situation meant that many soldiers were unmoved, fighting for survival rather than for the Fatherland. One *SS* Grenadier wrote: 'Morale is being completely destroyed by warfare in the East. We are told to fight to the death, but we no longer have the manpower resources or strength to wage such a war'.

RIGHT: A 3.7cm (1.45in) Flak gun mounted on an Sd.Kfz.7/1 half-track opens fire against attacking Soviet aircraft. The final battle before Berlin began at dawn on 16 April 1945, just 61km (38 miles) east of the German capital above the swollen River Oder. At this critical moment, the majority of the best *Waffen-SS* divisions were far to the south, retreating for their lives through Austria, the South and West. Of the many units that were trying in vain to prop up the disintegrating Eastern Front, only a handful were of top quality. These had been scraped together in a newly established 11th *Panzer* Army under the command of *SS Obergruppenführer* Felix Steiner. Hitler, living in a fantasy world, ordered Steiner's army to launch an offensive aimed at outflanking and then cutting off the Red Army advance on Berlin.

ABOVE: An Sd.Kfz. 251 half-track and motorcycle pass through improvized defences in an eastern German town. Soldiers and civilians have used destroyed vehicles to bar the route, though such barricades would not last long against T-34s or the masssive new Joseph Stalin heavy tank. Fortifying German towns was not easy. There were almost no mines, which were essential to making a defensive position, and even barbed wire had become almost impossible to obtain. Instead, there were masses of steel anti-tank obstacles, lorries and tramcars filled with stones. These were to be used to block main approaches when the city came under attack. 'It will take the Reds at least two hours and fifteen minutes to break-through', a joke went: 'Two hours laughing their heads off and fifteen minutes smashing the barricades'. Nothing could stop the Soviet juggernaut. The end had come to all the armed services of Hitler's once powerful Reich.

LEFT: A Marder II in action. Armed with the excellent 7.62cm (3in) Pak 36 (r) gun, one of hundreds captured from the Soviets in 1941 and 1942, this improvised light tank hunter proved to be highly effective, whether mounted on captured French chassis or on obsolete Panzer II or Panzer 38(t) platforms. Whatever the origins of the carrier, mounted atop was a high, box-like, 14.5mm (¹/₂in) thick armoured superstructure with steeply sloping sides. The Marder proved very popular among the *Waffen-SS* troops, and their immediate battlefield success in the East led to additional conversions. Some 531 Marder II served in the *SS* divisional anti-tank battalions until the very last months of the war.

ABOVE: Retreating across the snow in early March 1945, *SS Panzergrenadiers* hitch a lift onboard a StuG.III Ausf. G self-propelled gun. Riding on the hull of armoured vehicles was one of the most efficient ways in which grenadiers could be transported into battle: riding in the open rather than in trucks meant that they could get into action immediately. In attack, when the tank approached the objective area the *Panzergrenadiers* dismounted from the vehicle. Their task was to scout ahead of the armour to guard against enemy counterattacks as the *Panzers* punched their way through the enemy defences. However, by 1945, the grenadiers were being used in small mobile groups of *SS* tanks and were constantly 'fire brigaded', being moved from one danger spot to another. One advantage was that riding a tank was warm – at least if you were on the tank's engine decking at the rear rather than taking the wind in the teeth at the front.

**ABOVE:** Some of the armoured vehicles scraped together for Steiner's Eleventh *Panzer* Army. An Sd.Kfz.250 can be seen, armed with a 7.5cm (2.95in) KwK L/24 gun. When the final Russian offensive was launched on 16 April 1945, Steiner's force only had three reliable divisions. One of these, the 18th *Panzergrenadier* Division, was transferred to the front lines east of Berlin. Days later, the 11th *SS Panzergrenadier* Division *Nordland* was rushed to the Reich capital, whilst the *SS Brigade Nederland* was transferred to the south of the city to help prevent any possible Red Army breakthrough. Deep in his bunker, Adolf Hitler was still moving divisions about on a map, unaware that most had been broken in the fight with the Soviets. Hitler's staff issued orders to armies which no longer existed, to commanders who were already in contact with the Allies, and to party members who were mostly fleeing westwards ahead of the Red Army. The last defence of the Reich was left in the hands of the old and the young of Berlin, leavened by a few fanatical *SS* men and foreign volunteers.

**RIGHT:** *Waffen-SS* troops on the Vistula Front in early March 1945. A Pz.Kpfw.IV Ausf. H moves through the snow in support of its troops. Note how the tank stands out without the application of whitewash camouflage paint. During March, *Wehrmacht* and *Waffen-SS* troops could barely holding the wavering Vistula defences that ran some 280km (175 miles) from the Baltic coast to the juncture of the Oder and Neisse in Silesia. Most of the front was now held on the western bank of the Oder. In the north, the ancient city of Stettin, capital of Pomerania, and in the south the town of Küstrin were vital strongpoints guarding the flanks of the final Russian objective of the war – Berlin. The Western Allies had given up the race for the *Reich* capital, so the defenders knew that, somehow, they must prevent the Red Army from breaking through their positions and driving headlong into the very heart of the Homeland.

## WAFFEN-SS RANKS AND THEIR ENGLISH EQUIVALENTS

| | |
|---|---|
| *SS-Schütze* | Private |
| *SS-Oberschütze* | Senior Private, attained after six months' service |
| *SS-Sturmmann* | Lance-Corporal |
| *SS-Rottenführer* | Corporal |
| *SS-Unterscharführer* | Senior Corporal/Lance-Sergeant |
| *SS-Scharführer* | Sergeant |
| *SS-Oberscharführer* | Staff Sergeant |
| *SS-Hauptscharführer* | Warrant Officer |
| *SS-Sturmscharführer* | Senior Warrant Officer after 15 years' service |
| *SS-Untersturmführer* | Second Lieutenant |
| *SS-Obersturmführer* | First Lieutenant |
| *SS-Hauptsturmführer* | Captain |
| *SS-Sturmbannführer* | Major |
| *SS-Oberbannsturmführer* | Lieutenant-Colonel |
| *SS-Standartenführer* | Colonel |
| *SS-Oberführer* | Senior Colonel |
| *SS-Brigadeführer* und *Generalmajor der Waffen-SS* | Major-General |
| *SS-Gruppenführer* und *Generalleutnant der Waffen-SS* . | Lieutenant-General |
| *SS-Obergruppenführer* und *General der Waffen-SS* | General |
| *SS-Oberstgruppenführer* und *Generaloberst der Waffen-SS* | Colonel-General |
| *Reichsführer-SS* | (no English equivalent) |